Wicca is a form of positive witchcraft based on the love of nature and ancient spirituality. It is not a hidden, secret art, fit only for clandestine gatherings of weird people. Wicca is the magic found in our everyday lives, and if we open our eyes and learn to identify and use it for our own benefit, we will be taking our first step into an enchanted world

Day-By-Day

Wicca

Tabatha Jennings

Astrolog Publishing House

P. O. Box 1123, Hod Hasharon 45111, Israel
Tel: 972-9-7412044
Fax: 972-9-7442714
E-Mail: info@astrolog.co.il
Astrolog Web Site: www.astrolog.co.il

ISBN 965-494-108-2

Published by Astrolog Publishing House 2001

Printed in Israel
10 9 8 7 6 5 4 3 2 1

Introduction

The traditional definition of wicca is: Wicca is "witchcraft" in the framework of religion. It is a pagan religion that worships the goddess (mainly) and God.

Wicca today, called modern wicca or New Age wicca, is characterized by two main features: there are practical results (following a wicca action, that is, a transaction between the spiritual world and the material world), and there is a great deal of flexibility in it, that is, adaptation to traditions and various methods and ways of operation.

It can be said that in addition to those two features, wicca activity has seven characteristics that have caused it to be popular and to spread throughout the world. These seven characteristics are:

1. Equality between male and female.

2. Activity in a "circle" - everyone is equal, no one sits at "the head of the table."

3. Every contribution or opinion of every individual is considered.

4. Person power (material) is combined with the spirituality of the individual.

5. There is no dogma or strict doctrine.

6. There is no hierarchy.

7. Iron rule: "Do as you please - as long as you do not hurt anyone else."

Some people see wicca as the fastest growing religion in England and the United States. There are people who claim that it is a cult that is seeking to undermine Christianity, and reckon that it is marginal only. Some people see it as the leading New Age movement, while others see it as the expression of the religious cult of obvious supporters of the quality of the environment.

Although there is a certain element of truth in each of these views, they do not have much in common with the real essence of wicca, nor do they explain what wicca is.

Wicca, as a religion and a way of life, is generally not properly understood. The aim of this book is to clarify the practice and the main beliefs of wicca, and present its manifestations in everyday life - as they are seen and experienced in the eyes of the author of the book.

Modern wicca has only been in existence for about 80 years, and it can be said that it was given the impetus for its renewed thriving at the end of the First World War, when many of the foundations of society, which had existed since the Middle Ages, were undermined and underwent change. Wiccans are known as "good witches" and "good wizards" today. (While reading the book, you will become aware that I place great emphasis on the words "witches" and "wizards," that is, women who deal in witchcraft and men who deal in witchcraft. The purpose of this is to stress the fact that both sexes are active in the field of wicca.) However, wicca involves much more than white magic. In fact, picturesque "white magic" is actually "self-awareness work" (since it is focused on self-work and refrains from interfering in other people's lives and from manipulating other people's desires in any way). Today's witches and wizards are mostly ordinary people whose beliefs derive from the ancient roots of the traditional, rustic (and pagan) pre-Christian culture, and are adapted to the needs of modern life.

Wicca develops and changes when new supporters come along and adopt it, so that wicca today is different than the wicca of 80 years ago or the wicca of 20 years ago. As a result, modern wicca consists of many components, so that it is difficult to give it a clear and succinct definition. There are many fundamental beliefs, but wicca is also what every individual brings to it and creates from it.

The New Age movement in the second half of the 20th century, which was preceded by the occultism of the first half of the century, caused the many ideas and beliefs of wicca to become a central current in society and thought. Today, you can go to almost any bookstore and buy a deck of Tarot cards, and astrologers and soothsayers are really numerous among lawyers. Various workshops reveal the feminine aspect of godhood, the goddess, and Robert Graves' book, The White Goddess, has become a bestseller decades after its appearance on the book market. Centers for the study of Shamanism attract many seekers. Although all those are not pure wicca, they all include fundamentals of wicca.

You are almost certainly confused about the question of what actually is wicca, and what is not wicca. Don't worry - you'll be confused after reading this book, too! The various traditions are numerous and contradictory, as is the path a person chooses to perform his work, and even the goddess or god he chooses to believe in. Remember - no one can put together your art of white magic for you! The only thing that can be done is to offer ways and ideas. The work is yours entirely.

What is wicca?

Wicca is a modern version of the original pre-Christian Shaman tradition. It is a pagan religion, that is, a religion that is not Judeo-Christian in origin. The word "pagan" comes from the Latin root, paganus, which means "not of a city" or, in other words, rustic. Since Christianity spread very slowly in outlying rustic regions, the faith (which was "Christian," ultimately) became a mixture of old and new religions among the pagans. Many local saints are actually the christianized versions of pagan gods that were adopted so that the locals would accept the Christian faith more easily.

Wicca involves the earth, nature, and fertility. Its adherents celebrate the changes of the seasons and the new and full moon. In that sense, wicca is similar to astrology, except that the festivals that are celebrated in it do not derive from the individual birth map, but rather from the life cycle of the earth and the universe (the longest day of the year, the longest night of the year, and so on). Wicca believers, in general, recognize male and female gods alike, and believe in reincarnation, magic, and soothsaying. Wicca is actually a spiritual and philosophical path, but it is also a religion, called a "craft," which means the craft of the wise.

The word wicca comes from two possible sources. The first is the Anglo-Saxon "wic" or "wit," which means "wise" or "learned." A person "of wicca" was a person who had acquired knowledge (especially of healing and plants) that differentiated him from the ordinary people. "Wicka" is the title of the wise witch or wizard who acquired knowledge that was not accessible to everyone. Another possible source is the Celtic word "wick," which means "to bend" or "to be flexible." According to the Celtic tradition, the wicca people were those who bent themselves to the various demands of life and circumstances. In the story of the oak and the willow, the oak does not bend, and is uprooted by the storm. The willow, on the other hand, being pliant, bends, and thus survives the storm with minor damage. In other cultures, this principle appears in the form of a reed instead of the willow.

Wicca is a unique religion in that it lacks a doctrine that is imposed by a hierarchical structure, and it does not provide a law or holy book (such as the Bible or the Koran) that wiccans can consult in order to obtain spiritual guidance. (This is the reason why there is no "right" or "wrong" wicca book, and alongside a great deal of similarity between various wicca books, you will also find many significant differences.) In contrast, wicca contains different traditions, and this means that it enables individuals to work by themselves, and assumes that every individual will develop and continue to relate to his or her basic or prior set of beliefs and spiritual work.

However, even personal work tends to be influenced by the work of the other "witches" and "wizards" with whom the person is in contact, or by sources that are different than the ones from which the person learned the fundamentals of wicca. If a person lives in a region in which there are several groups with wiccan characteristics, or if he studied from several sources, he has a broader range of choice. If there is only one small group that becomes a role model (or just one source of knowledge), there is a danger of a limited point of view - instead of the broadness and the variety that characterize wicca. From this, it is clear that it is preferable to broaden one's point of view and "bake" a personal "wicca cake" from as many "ingredients" as possible.

Ultimately, wicca practitioners work individually.

Most of the witches and wizards are actually "ordinary people," even though they are more "spiritual" than the average person.

Witches and wizards must think for themselves and choose and develop ways of action and beliefs of their own, and each of them can quit a particular group or trend at a certain stage and create a "wicca group" of his own. Thus, wicca is not a religion that traps individuals, but rather individuals drop out and create a current or a large movement together. Having said this, witches and wizards still have something in common with one another (more than differences), and they get together at festivals, ceremonies, and wicca conferences called sabbats. Despite all the differences of opinion that frequently emerge among different groups of wicca practitioners, it is important to remember how much they have in common. The principles and beliefs mentioned at the beginning, sometimes called "The Seven Pillars of Wicca," are common to most of the groups that engage in wicca.

It is possible to learn about the wicca sources from myths and from beliefs that are sometimes called superstitions (some of which are presented in the book). I believe that various superstitions, from the black cat that crosses your path to entering the sports field right foot first, are nothing but manifestations of traditional wicca beliefs or customs that have been preserved. It is easier for a person to knock three times on a wooden table in order to prevent bad luck than to go to the forest and embrace an oak tree - the traditional wicca method of dispelling bad luck. For this reason, I present many beliefs in this book, from love spells to "superstitions" that have become accepted. In some of these, I will also explain the connection to wicca. I also recommend that the reader refer to the sources of the wicca traditions, such as Robert Graves' book, The White Goddess. The modern form of wicca is a mixture of ceremonial witchcraft, theosophy, mysticism, spiritual movements, principles of religions in the West and in the East, western and eastern philosophies, mythologies, folk tales, and legends, superstitions, and various arts of soothsaying. Some of the traditions are "pure" pagan, based on the pre-Christian traditions only (from Europe and the Mediterranean basin), and others blend gnostic, eastern, and other motifs.

As I said before, this book presents customary and accepted witchcraft, which is considered to be white magic - that is, performed in the framework of accepted wicca.

The rose of love

The man yearns for the young woman, the woman yearns for the handsome young man - what do they do? How do they fulfill their love?

Among many European nations - the Italians, the Romanians, the Greeks, and the Gypsies - we find a spell in which the rose, preferably a red one, is used for this purpose.

This is what the amorous man - or woman - has to do:

1. Select a fresh, half-open red rose. If you pluck the rose from the bush with your own hands, do it at sunset. (In an ancient book of Greek origin, there is an additional warning: if the lover is pricked by the thorns of the rose, and a drop of blood falls on the ground, he should throw the rose to the ground and wait eight days before repeating the procedure. So, dear readers and lovers of spells, be careful of thorns!)

2. Purchase or prepare three tall, red candles. (If you use candles scented with aromatic fragrances, you should go for a jasmine-scented candle.)

3. Before going to sleep, place the rose in a glass of water or a vase next to your bed. With the three candles, create a triangle around the glass or vase containing the rose.

4. Go to sleep... and try to dream about your beloved the whole night.

5. At dawn - it's very important that you do this before the sun rises - position the rose so that it is facing east to greet the rising sun. You must stick the stem of the rose into a pile of sand in a glass or an empty jar, or in a flowerpot filled with sand. The rose can be placed on the windowsill, the roof, or in the yard.

6. Now take two of the red candles from the triangle surrounding the rose, stand them on either side of the rose, and light them.

7. While the candles are burning, think about your beloved in your heart and say aloud: "This red rose is the messenger of true love. These candles will convey my love to my beloved's heart..." and think about his/her name without saying it aloud.

8. Now return the rose to its place next to your bed (not in a glass or vase containing water) and (carefully!) put the burning candles in next to it. Let the candles burn down.

9. Leave the rose and the remains of the candles (the wax) in the same place for three days and three nights.

10. On the morning of the fourth day, take the withered rose petals, the remnants of wax from the burnt-down candles, and the third, whole, candle. Place all of this in a cloth or red paper bag.

11. Bury the bag in a hole you have dug in the ground, and cover the hole well.

12. And now, all you have to do is to go and phone or send a letter or e-mail to the person on whose behalf you have gone to so much trouble.

If you read this spell carefully, you will notice that it contains different components of wicca (some of which you will come across later in the book): the use of a flower, that is, of our link with plants; emphasis on the color red, which is the central color in wicca (the color of blood, and also the color of menstruation, and defined as "the color of life" in many wicca groups); emphasis on the times of sunset and sunrise; emphasis on one of the directions of the winds (east); the use of the different elements - fire (by means of candles), water, earth (burial in the earth), wind (the sound of a plea); exploiting the dream in order to channel with the subconscious; the use of visualization (thinking about the object of the spell). We see that in a simple and accepted spell, there are many components, most of which you can find in the accepted ceremonies and beliefs in wicca groups... and still, many people use this love spell (which is defined as a superstition) under the impression that they are not engaging in wicca.

Cycles and rhythms

My first link with wicca occurred when I read an article on the great importance of the lunar cycle on life. In fact, the lunar cycles are the most important cycle in human life (especially for women) and for life on the earth where we live. Various witches and wizards claim that it is enough for us to adapt our body - both physical and spiritual - and the rhythm of our lives to the lunar cycle, and our lives will undergo an enormous change. I think that what all wicca groups have in common, all over the world, is the recognition of the lunar cycles and adapting the rituals and rhythm of life to these cycles.

This in-depth article was given to me as a gift of love by my good friend, Yvette R. Hofen, astrologer, wizard, and researcher of spells and enchantments in ancient cultures. With her permission, I will reveal it to the general public so that this important information can serve all of us in our everyday lives:

"The moon, the spinner of time, served as our natural clock before we submitted to the linear concept of time. The moon, knowing that it was still an illuminating eye in the nocturnal heavens, did not care. It knew that it still controlled the seasons, the tides, the floods, the crops, moods, the feminine cycle, human sexuality and energy levels - the list goes on and on.

The animals all obeyed it, as did the oceans and the plant

kingdom. The moon has all the time in the world to look at human beings with an ironic smile, since its time stands still and exists. We can choose to ignore it consciously, and go on living our lives according to linear time, but we will still be affected by the magnetic poles of the moon!

Lunar time is available to all of us, and it can be seen as something that can unite the whole world in a harmonious and synchronous rhythm, like one big orchestra.

Since our body is composed of a very high percentage of water, the biological and psychological cycles, sexual urges, moods, and passions inside us are influenced by the moon just as the oceans and the natural world outside of us are.

It is possible to see the moon's path in the heavens as a cyclical creation that renews itself, beginning with birth and going on to death, after which it is renewed. The path to awareness passes through a lack of awareness (no moon), from the unknown to knowledge and enlightenment.

Since water, which symbolizes the subconscious, constitutes 70% of the composition of our bodies, our moods fluctuate like the tide because of the magnetic influence of the moon.

The purpose of this table is to help increase our awareness of these cycles and of how they influence our lives personally.

Through the understanding of the lunar cycles, we illuminate the subconscious and learn to swim and flow harmoniously in its waters, instead of fighting the natural currents of the cycles.

The understanding of the lunar cycles and their influence on us will help us know what the best time is to begin new projects, make plans, kick inhibiting habits, fulfill obligations, work as hard as we can - or rest.

If we feel tired, lacking in energy and motivation, we can look up at the night sky, stare at the moon, peek at the table and check: if we discover that there is a new moon above us, we will have to accept what our body is trying to tell us - it's time to rest, and we must not push ourselves forward and cause an unnecessary expenditure of energy. If we are planning to begin a new project, we should look at the sky and see if the state of the moon and the energies that are influenced by it are giving us their support.

This is the "practical spell" for universal existence.

Originally, Yvette Hofen entrusted her writings to me. They were laid out in the form of a large circular table, without beginning or end. Her suggestion was to draw a large circle on a sheet of Bristol paper, and divide it into six "pizza triangles." Above each triangle, the moon as it appeared at that particular time of its cycle was to be drawn, and in each triangle, the significance of the state of the moon and its effect on us was to be written. The Bristol sheet should be hung in the home, in the study, for example, and should be consulted on a daily basis.

New moon

Full moon

New moon

The beginning of the moon's period of filling out. At this stage, we begin to see the thin crescent moon gradually filling out. In this period, the energies rise in a spiral upward from their source, and spread. This is a time of expansion and spreading, a time for great achievements, for making plans, for increasing energies and confidence in life. It is the stage of the potential, the hidden strength.

Stage 1

Stage 2

Revival, birth, existence

Birth and existence - through the gates of life (the vagina), light springs out of the darkness.

This is a time of rebirth, awakening from the deep sleep that the disappearance of the moon symbolizes, awakening from a deep sleep fresh and full of energies, ready for new adventures. You have the passion for growth and rapid development in you that characterizes the newborn. Your renewed appearance brings with it new energies and ideas. This is the time for sowing the seeds! Now decide which seeds you want to sow and get all the materials together in order to complete the project.

Lay the foundations, now, during this period.

Energies of growth, regeneration, pregnancy, creation, and fertility dance and skip in the universe, expand everything with which they come into contact, and create dissemination.

Everything grows easily, without effort.

Just decide what you want to create/realize and do it.

Start now!

Half moon - on the way to being full

We are in a period in which the first half of the moon is fully visible, and is advancing toward full moon.

Stage 3

Stage 4

Stage 5

We become serious people

This was created seven days ago, with the rebirth of the moon. In the last seven days, you spent your time making and creating new plans and ideas. Now the hard work begins.

Take positive actions in order to move forward fast and easily. Support yourself - with intention, with thought, with speech, and with action. If you move now, you will grow quickly.

The energies are high, you can achieve a lot if you focus and commit yourself with determination and persistence.

This is the time to complete the main body of work and leave the finishing touches and the work on the finer details to later.

Fight, overcome obstacles - be like a fighter, like an invincible Amazon, be strong and durable like cast concrete.

Full moon

Positive ions in the atmosphere following the electromagnetism of the spiral that spins upward from the earth.

Externalization of people's personalities, the full moon reveals what is hidden in the face.

Stage 6

Stage 7

Lunamania, lunatic, hysteria

What energies!

The energetic power is tremendous - flow with it!

Give yourself a pat on the back for your hard work and effort of the preceding days. Celebrate your power and wisdom by allowing yourself time to celebrate the full moon with friends and loved ones.

Dance, sing, play, drum, stay awake all night and celebrate the full moon outside, under the starry sky.

The fullness of the moon reflects the fullness of the power and spiritual strength that are available to us.

When the valleys of the emotional unknown are realized visibly, they become available for the use of the aware person.

The full moon brings enlightenment. The face of the truth is exposed - the truth whose light bursts forth fully now through the darkness.

This is the time to look inward, to survey your actions, feelings, and emotions of the preceding days, and discover the irrelevant subjects or criticisms you allowed to distract you and divert you from your main aim.

Focus and muster your full strength.

This is the time to make wishes for peace, prosperity, growth, love, success, harmony...

Speak to the big moon and bring the realization of your wishes down to earth with the help of its light.

Meditate to receive additional insights and to achieve additional illumination. The illumination you are acquiring now will help you complete your work and polish your ideas.

Beginning of the absent stage of the moon

Now the passage to the absent lunar stage begins, in which the energies move in a spiral downward, to the self, to the source. It is a time of return, closure, conclusion, and completion.

Stage 8

Stage 9

Maturation

At this point, the light of the full moon has exposed new secrets, illuminated processes and the course of tasks in your life, revealed hidden aspects both in your personality and in the tasks you have undertaken to complete this month / during your life, and shown you which parts of the plan still require polishing and completion. This means that with the help of your new-old knowledge and greater understanding, you know and understand what is happening, and have all the necessary tools to complete the tasks you have undertaken. This is a time of final and sometimes more difficult declarations.

Temptations and illusory perceptions lie in wait along the path, ready to lead you astray and divert you from the path along which you are going.

A process of plunging deeper and deeper into the dark realms of the soul is taking place.

Dormant negative energies that lay hidden behind fears are liable to reveal themselves now. If you are aware of this, you have an opportunity to overcome and conquer them, since you understood where they were hiding all along.

Because of the decrease in the rate of growth and

expansion, every success must come from your depths and the resources inside you.

There is a feeling of thickening, concentrations.

Continuation of the absent stages of the moon
Stage 10
Stage 11

Come to the "reaper"
Now the threatening old man arrives with his scythe in order to remove, destroy, liberate, clean, clarify, and separate.

This is your "funeral."

Let go of your fears and doubts and release them; let the detachment process occur peacefully. Don't fight it, and avoid unnecessary conflicts.

Rest...

Let the ropes become detached.

Break down negativity and discard it. Get rid of negative habits, destroy negative or unhealthy relationships, defuse hostile situations.

Let go!

The energies are decreasing, diminishing on their way to the source, so let what you don't need in your life decrease and go with them.

If objectives are not accomplished, or were not accomplished during preceding stages, this is the time to deliberate and ask "Why?" Instead of throwing yourself into hard work, work at getting rid of those inhibiting patterns.

Finish what can be finished now, and let other aims and objectives die, or leave them behind you in order to begin them again at the next stage.

Clean and purify your space. Wash clothes. Throw out anything you don't need.

The moon is not visible in the sky
The electromagnetic field moves down the spiral toward the earth, pulling everything back to the source.
Inward withdrawal
Stage 12

Stopping the world
After the last cycle, you're tired.

You've studied, worked, achieved, sprouted, grown.

The "reaper" has arrived and helped you clean and clarify the matters of this world, and now is the time to plunge back into the waters of life once more.

When the moon disappears for those three days, it takes you with it. As a dead soul, you are crawling back into its womb and waiting for rebirth.

Inside the womb, you become the wholeness of yourself. There you can gain memories and dreams of previous lives; there you can really know yourself.

This is the perfect time to enter your cave and "hibernate," stop the world, deliberate, meditate, sleep, rest, nurture yourself, dream.

Dip yourself in water: showers, pampering baths, mineral bath, a dip in the sea.

Light candles and incense.

Spend time on the shore.

Spend time in the heart of nature.

You must rest and burn old karma in order to prepare yourself for your renewed appearance.

Four principles of wicca

As we said before, wicca has a very small number of absolute laws, a small amount of doctrine, and a few guidelines of faith that are shared by wicca adherents. The four basic principles that guide wicca are distinguishing between the dark side and the light side of our lives, the law of three, the sentence about not hurting others, and the law of "do unto others as you would have others do unto you." These principles may seem somewhat simplistic, but remember that the simpler a rule is, the more appropriate it is to everyday life.

The dark/light side

This principle actually distinguishes between white magic, which belongs to wicca, and black magic, which I totally eschew. Most of the witches and wizards are aware of the existence of the "dark side," which is sometimes liable to contain "evil." In general, what is considered to be "light" is what is positive and beneficial, constructive and creative. What is considered to be "dark" is what is harmful, injurious, and destructive. This can be seen as creation as opposed to destruction. However, instead of identifying everything dark with evil, the witches and wizards understand that the dark side is an integral part of the universe.

To a certain extent, there is a return to the first days of the various godheads. In the beginning, God was good and evil together - He could create man but also expel him from the

Garden of Eden; He could save mankind from the flood but also destroy it at Sodom and Gemorrah. God contained both the light side and the dark side. Over time, God began to be perceived as "light" only, pure, whose deeds were all for the good. And what is the connection to the dark side he had? It was transferred to Satan, and two camps were formed - the light camp of God and the dark camp of Satan and the demons. Wicca is directed at the light camp. Whoever does not understand and apply this principle does not belong in a pure wicca group. We are well aware that in everything in the universe (including God), there is a light part and a dark part - but we focus solely on the light part, and try to nurture and increase it tenfold. We ignore or pay as little attention as possible to the dark part.

Some people claimed that witches and wizards "worship Satan." Satan first appears in the Jewish religion as an angel who defied God and plummeted from heaven to earth. In the beginning, since God was both good and evil, there was in fact no need for Satan. After God became absolute good, his antithesis - Satan, absolute evil - was required. Remember that the idea of the devil developed in the early Christian traditions. Since wicca is not a religion (Jewish or Christian), but rather a natural set of beliefs, it does not relate to Satan. Satan is not a part of wicca, which is based on the connection to nature and on the beliefs linked to nature in the way it existed before the spread of Christianity (that is, pagan beliefs).

It is important to stress that wiccans relate with respect and patience to other channels of spiritual development and to faiths that are different than theirs (including belief in the devil) - in the same way as they would want others to relate to their beliefs.

The body, for instance, contains both anabolic (constructive) and catabolic (destructive) processes, which maintain its balance and the natural process of life-death-life. Compost, for example, rots and breaks down (rot and breakdown represent the dark side), but the rotting and breakdown of the compost are life-giving and nurture the soil. Death is a dark process, but it is an integral part of life. Witches and wizards respect death as a natural part of the cycle. For this reason, they prefer to think of the dark side as a natural side of life, and not to fear or deny it, but rather to understand and respect it because of its natural function.

Evil is something else. Destruction and death are natural process, but when they occur as actions in the service of a particular human objective, they belong to the definition of "evil." For this reason, some people see evil as an expression of intent. When a volcano erupts and devastates its surroundings, it belongs to the "dark" side, but it is also a natural force that does not stem from evil intent. However, when a plane is flown into a huge office building, this is a situation that belongs to the definition of evil. Even more important than the action itself is the intent.

Every act of intentional harm to people or animals (such as animal sacrifice) is "evil." In other words, evil is an intentional human action, and not a natural action. Every such action is unequivocally eschewed by the witches and wizards of wicca.

The law of three

"Everything you do will come back to you threefold." The law of three does not just relate to witchcraft and spells, but serves as a way to oversee everyday conduct. This means that if you radiate love, it will come back to you threefold, and if you radiate hostility or negativity, it will come back to you threefold. This is the law that prevents wiccans from "cursing" others. Since wiccans use spells and witchcraft, the possibility of using these means for negative purposes exists. The witches and wizards are well aware of what "black magic" is, and because of the law of three, they avoid it at any cost. Most wicca "spells" are used for self-development, and are not as they are shown in various movies about witches, where the witch crooks a finger or mumbles a spell, and her wish is granted immediately. These are not attained by wiccans.

I would like to point out that the number three is arbitrary. I chose this number since it contains the combination of woman + man + offspring, and therefore relates to the idea of growth. Some people prefer the number five (pentagram), and then the principle is defined as the "law of five." Others prefer the number seven ("the law of seven"), which is the mystical number that has the greatest influence. Yet others choose the number nine ("the law of nine"), which is the number that contains the entire universe, in their opinion.

The "do not hurt" sentence

"Do as you please - as long as you do not hurt anyone else."

This sentence is in fact the main guiding principle of wicca activity. It states that you may do as you please as long as you do not hurt anyone else - including yourself.

This rule means that the person must always be aware of the consequences of every deed, and how it affects others. The word "others" does not only refer to people who the person knows or does not know, but also to nature, to "Mother Earth," and to the members of her family - the plant, animal, and mineral kingdoms.

Most witches and wizards weigh up every action before they actually perform it. If any damage is liable to be caused, they assess the level of damage and then select a manner of action that will not cause damage.

Upholding the "do not hurt" sentence leads naturally to an "ecological" way of life. The person may well become a "green," become a different kind of consumer in order to generate less refuse and pollution, maintain good neighborly relations, and so on.

What causes "damage" or "harm" to Mother Earth is a central topic of interest and conversation in wicca groups. In the main, people agree that "damage" or "harm" includes negative actions, actions that have a deleterious effect on others or on oneself. Occasionally, a lack of action is also liable to cause tremendous damage.

Do unto others as you would have them do unto you

This sentence belongs to the Judeo-Christian biblical tradition. It is a simple rule that appears in various forms in most cultures. This sentence is similar to the "do not hurt" sentence, and it is a good guideline to live by. As we said above, it appears in different versions in various cultures: "Don't do anything to your friend that you yourself hate having done to you," or "If you have been burnt by fire, don't throw burning embers on your friend," and so on.

This law causes the person to think about his actions and take responsibility for them. Witches and wizards do not enjoy the convenience of "confession" or forgiveness for crimes, as in other religions. They are supposed to take responsibility for their actions and face the consequences of their deeds and mistakes. If they make a mistake, they examine what they did and why they did it, in order to be more aware and avoid mistakes in the future. If possible, they repair their deeds in the present.

Wicca - from birth to death (and after death)

In this chapter, you have already become acquainted with the lunar cycles, which are so important in wicca. Now we will meet the life cycle itself and the various rituals - or key points - that are connected to it.

Since wicca responds to the cyclical aspect of nature, the different stages of man's life cycle are also emphasized, and appear in various rites of passage. The main stages that are accepted by most wicca practitioners can be identified.

Wiccaning - the name-giving ceremony

Wiccaning, or name-giving, is the term used to describe the festivities that attend the birth of a child. Since wicca is essentially a fertility religion, the birth of a child is perceived as a gift from the gods and as a sacred rite in itself. After the birth of the child, when the life of the family has returned to normal, the parents and community celebrate the wiccaning of the child, giving it a name that will protect it during its growth and development. There is no fixed age or format for the name-giving ceremony - it can occur during the baptism, the brit milah (Jewish circumcision ceremony), or any ceremony that is not connected to a religion and is mainly pagan. It must be remembered that wicca is a religion of choice, and although the child receives a name, he/she is entitled to choose his/her own spiritual path or religion upon reaching maturity - as well as to change his/her name!

The ceremony performed upon reaching sexual maturity

In wicca, reaching sexual maturity is extremely important, especially in groups of women, when a young girl has her first period and becomes a woman. The women get together for a celebration or a party in honor of the girl, and on this occasion, the girl hears about the responsibility that accompanies sexual maturity. Since free choice is of great importance in wicca, the girl has the option of being sexually active. It is important to remember that although fertility is the central belief in wicca, this does not include sexual promiscuity (as it does in various black magic rites - for example the ones recommended by Alistair Crawley). The opposite is true - personal responsibility and free choice in the sexual realm lead to aware sexual relations that are also linked to love and partnership.

The time for celebrating boys' sexual maturity is not defined. It can be upon the appearance of the secondary sex characteristics such as the growth of a mustache and pubic hair, or when the boy makes a conscious choice to undertake the responsibility of a man (like the Jewish bar-mitzvah ceremony). The tradition of celebrating boys' sexual maturity is not widespread in wicca. At such parties, if they are held, the boy is told about sexual responsibility and his obligations upon reaching maturity.

The witches and wizards consider sexuality to be a natural and normal part of human life. How sexuality manifests itself is a totally private matter, so long as the person expresses his sexuality in accordance with the law of wicca that states: "Do as you please - as long as you do not hurt anyone else."

For witches and wizards, the family is sacred. However, their definition of "family" may extend beyond merely their nuclear family: family can also be the extended family of grandparents, aunts and uncles, and cousins. It can also include the members of the group, friends, the High Priestess or the High Priest, and so on. There are witches and wizards who consider all the witches and wizards in the world as one big family.

Initiation rites

Initiation is an important part of the rites of passage. For the most part, initiation does not only indicate a stage of learning or achievement, but also accompanies or inspires inner change. Initiation bears a somewhat mystical nature, and it is performed when the person shows signs of inner discovery or a deep inner change.

Initiation rites may differ slightly from tradition to tradition, but the rite is just the outer manifestation of the initiation. Personal experience is what counts, and this must be experienced personally.

Since the name-giving alone does not guarantee that the person will become a witch/wizard, it is necessary for the person to opt to "practice" in order to receive initiation. The first stage in initiation is consecration. This is the obligation to learn about the wicca that the person applies to himself, to the community, and to the goddess and god. If the person is committed to consecration, it attests to a certain level of commitment, but does not yet attest to total membership, as initiation does. It is generally accepted that at least a year and a day must elapse between consecration and initiation. This time is devoted to studying the principles and practice of wicca, including the practice of (white) magic. An important part of initiation is learning the group's technical "language," so that the person can communicate easily with others of the same tradition.

There is no specific age when initiation is permitted, even though many groups do not permit minors to join a group that practices wicca actively. A 15-year-old may be knowledgeable and mature enough to choose a religious or spiritual path, but his parents and society are liable to forbid him to implement his will actively.

When the person studies wicca, there are three stages or three possible initiations. It is commonly said that "the initiates of the first stage are responsible for themselves; the initiates of the second stage are responsible for the cell/coven or group; and the initiates of the third stage are responsible for the community, for the whole." Every group and tradition has its own definitions, levels of study and specialization for each stage. The minimum time for progressing from the first stage to the second stage and from the second stage to the third stage varies, but it is accepted practice to wait at least a year and a day between stages.

Not all witches and wizards attain all three stages, but ideally a wicca practitioner has practiced and studied at least for the first stage. Wicca is a religion of "priests," that is, everyone who gets through initiation is considered to be a priest or priestess as a right and not as a favor, and is fully capable of communicating with the god directly.

In various wicca traditions, the title "High Priest" or "High Priestess" is given only to people who have attained the third stage of initiation. In other traditions, the title is used for the leader of the cell/coven.

The joining hands ceremony (marriage)

Joining hands is a rite of passage that occurs when an individual seeks to join his life with that of a partner in the eyes of God. This can include (lawful) marriage or deciding upon any other kind of couple relationship. Witches and wizards have various perceptions of committed relationships, including partnerships between people of the same sex. Witches and wizards sometimes have a committed polygamous relationship, even though this is rare.

Joining hands can last for a defined time-span (a year and a day, for instance) or it can last "until death do us part."

Joining hands is celebrated in much the same way as a wedding, with all the splendor that can be seen at modern weddings. Witches and wizards hold the ceremony in a circle. The couple takes a mutual oath, and occasionally their hands are tied together as a symbol of partnership. Afterwards, they may "jump over the broomstick" together, symbolizing the home they will share. (Jumping over the broomstick was an old English custom for ensuring that a couple was lawfully wedded if they lacked the money to register officially for marriage.)

The separating hands ceremony (divorce)

Separating hands is the ritual used by witches and wizards to signal divorce (or the termination of a committed relationship). Since joining hands is an enchanted ritual, the ritual for the termination of the relationship must also be enchanted. Often it is not possible to bring both members of the couple to the separating hands ritual, but when it can be done, the ritual leads to the termination and the closing of a circle.

The separating hands ceremony is performed in a circle, and the hands, which were joined together, are parted. This serves to untie the emotional and mystical knot binding the couple, so that each of them can continue his/her life free of the other one's influence. They are free to choose their own paths. Sometimes the ritual is followed by a party and a feast, sometimes not. It is best if the priest/ess who officiated at the joining hands ceremony also officiates at the separating hands ceremony.

The ceremony marking old age

The ceremony marking old age is a relatively important rite of passage in the wicca tradition. In recent centuries, society has pushed old people aside when they became useless economically. In contrast, wicca respects and appreciates people who have lived and studied for many years, and are now an asset to the wicca community. Wiccans who have practiced the craft for more than a generation are highly esteemed. They become the wise advisors to the active leaders. They tell stories of the past, of how things were in their youth, and share their knowledge and wisdom with the rest of the community. They are honored for their achievements and experience.

The ceremony marking old age is also performed for those who belonged to the community for many years and assumed the job of elders of the community (even if they were not old). It is sometimes performed for a woman who reaches menopause.

The ceremony marking old age is identical to the name-giving ceremony - festivities that celebrate the person's existence and his place in the wicca community. The ceremony is also perceived as a kind of initiation, even though it is not an initiation at a specific stage.

The ceremony marking old age can also indicate the time when a person retires from active leadership and assumes an advisory position in the circle of elders.

Rite of passage to the afterworld

Death is the last stage of life experienced by every person. Witches and wizards consider death a natural part of life. (A certain type of reincarnation constitutes a part of the wicca beliefs, and most wicca adherents also believe in reincarnation.) Many witches and wizards opt to go through this rite of passage some time before their actual death. If a person is dying, the witches and wizards visit him, speak to him, and make "peace" with him.

The person who is about to die must not be anxious or fearful about reaching the final initiation. The witches and wizards will feel sad about the imminent loss, but will also be full of hope for repose in "paradise," the place where witches and wizards go between one life and the next. This place is thought to be a place of eternal summer, warm, green, and pleasant. The souls of those who have already died are there and welcome the new arrival.

The dead are still with us in spirit and can be embodied among the living in a variety of ways. Many witches and wizards believe in life after death. The person who is about to die tries to make peace with the world and prepares himself for the imminent transition.

The ideal situation is for the witch's or wizard's transition to death to begin before actually dying, so that the person who is about to die can take part in this ritual or express his last wishes in this world, as well as make peace with and part from his relatives and friends. (The wicca tradition is greatly influenced by the principles of The Tibetan Book of the Dead regarding this topic. I recommend that every reader read the full version of The Tibetan Book of the Dead and think about it.)

The "burial" ceremony of the dead/ Remembering the dead

The memorial ceremonies of the witches and wizards are not as defined as the other rites of passage. Death is a natural part of life. Witches and wizards celebrate the secrets of death every year at Samhain, so that there is already an annual period of lamentation between the eight customary sabbats. The wicca memorial ceremony may be held in a circle in which the participants sing mystical songs and celebrate the cyclical nature of life and death. In certain groups, each person in the circle says a few words about the deceased. There are prayers for an easy passage to and a pleasant sojourn in "paradise." In cases of sudden death, there is liable to be extrasensory trauma. In such cases, the person may need assistance in his passage to the next world. The group tries to help the soul's journey to "paradise" by means of prayers and the energy of love.

It is rare for a witch or wizard to be buried openly as a witch or wizard. Frequently, the secrecy surrounding the person's role of witch or wizard causes the ceremony to be performed clandestinely.

Witches and wizards do not have a clear preference for burial or cremation. Since they perceive the body as a "vehicle" only and as the soul as the main factor, few of them consider the method of burial to be of significance.

It makes no difference at what time of year the death of the witch or wizard occurs; they will be remembered the following Samhain, since that is the purpose of that festival - to remember the dead.

When people begin to engage in wicca, they realize that the most difficult part is not learning the lunar or solar cycles, or the various ceremonies. The most difficult part is linking up to Mother Earth, or "grounding." In other words, it is much easier to learn the theories than to detach oneself - physically, spiritually, and emotionally - from the world in which we live, and link up to Mother Earth.

In order to engage in wicca in a beneficial manner, we must learn to perform the link to Mother Earth. Without this link, we will not be successful in any practical wicca ceremony.

The link to the earth is connected to another topic that is known to many today - the aura. The aura is the body of electromagnetic energy that surrounds the physical body and penetrates it. This aura is actually what we use in activating wicca and in grounding. In order to succeed in wicca activities, we need a clean and energetic aura.

Although I do not intend to discuss the aura and the maintenance of its energy here, I will present several useful methods (used in the wicca groups I lead) for cleansing the aura. This cleansing of the aura can be done before or after the act of grounding.

Ankh

The ankh is a special symbol, somewhat similar to a cross, which originated in the hieroglyphics of ancient Egypt. The meaning of the concept is "life." In etchings and paintings, we can see that the pharaohs are holding this symbol in their hands. In Egyptian literature, the symbol is also called "the key of life."

Today, the ankh is considered to be a sign with unique power, not particularly as an omen of life, but more in the sexual realm. (The sign of the ankh is in fact the basis of the symbol of Venus in astrology). The symbol is supposed to reinforce the person's sexuality, and many people have an ankh tattooed next to or on their genitals.

In Greece, the sign had a slightly different meaning. It is similar to the letter T, which indicates life, and when it is inverted, it signifies eternity. That is, eternal life.

Today, the ankh appears in jewelry and numerous ornaments, especially jewelry worn around the neck.

Grounding

Grounding is one of the most widespread spiritual exercises. Put simply, the idea behind grounding is to link us to the earth, something which is essential for people who are interested in wicca. Grounding to the earth enables us to get rid of excess energy and strengthens the link between us and the earth, which is our current place of residence. We need this link, since without it we cannot exist in the physical layer. When we begin to get involved in wicca, grounding becomes even more important.

Grounding helps us have our head in the clouds safely while we pick up divine messages and insights, and if our feet are planted firmly on the ground, we tread firmly in the material world.

Quick grounding exercise

This is a quick and simple exercise, and after you practice it a few times, you can apply it to every situation and place, even in crowded public places, by means of your visualization ability.

Stand or sit comfortably. Take several deep breaths and relax your body slightly if it is tense. If it is more comfortable for you, close your eyes. Concentrate on the region of your root chakra - the area between the anus and the genitals. See the root chakra as a spinning red wheel. From the chakra, see a thick red ray of light that splits into two thick, stable stripes of red light, each one flowing through one of your legs. The red light flows along your legs to your feet, penetrates the earth, and enters the bowels of the earth. Focus on this sight and on the feeling of the red light that has penetrated the bowels of the earth for a few minutes and say aloud or mentally: "All the energies I no longer need are descending to the bowels of the earth and are turning into positive energies."

When we say "are turning," we mean the earth's transformational ability to convert one form of energy into another, just as it is able to convert one substance into another - substances that are compounded and rot in it subsequently turn into nourishing substances for various plants and organisms. At the end of the meditation, it is also possible to see in the mind's eye a tall, strong tree coming out of the earth somewhere. Incidentally, the understanding of the earth's transformational ability and the tremendous importance of this ability will evoke in every aware person sincere concern for the children of the earth - the trees and the plants - which, regrettably, totally obtuse and unaware people tend to disregard. Awareness of Mother Earth and her children is an inseparable part of conscious awakening, and an important tool for any person who is involved in the occult and the supernatural. When you take care of the earth and its children, they will teach you marvelous secrets of the universe, if only you listen to them. Therefore, it is every enlightened person's cosmic duty to make sure, as far as possible, to raise other people's consciousness and actively fight against the obtuse and ugly exploitation and destruction that are occurring on earth. The very fact of your cerebral objection to the continuation of this exploitation, and your personal prayer for the welfare of the earth, will increase the critical mass that can stop the terrible destruction before it is too late (the destruction of the rainforests of Brazil is a clear example of how the greed for mammon leads to the devastation of our planet; let's hope that the rape of the forests will stop for the sake of Mother Earth's and our own health).

Contact with the earth

This simple grounding exercise is suitable for many people, and can easily be applied every time you feel a bit ungrounded.

Go outside and bend down to the earth, bending your knees slightly. Touch the bare earth with your hands for a few minutes. If you feel a need for it, dig your fingers deep into it, and be aware that you are releasing all your unneeded excess energies. Sometimes you can clearly feel the breakdown of the excess energy, or a feeling of release. If you want, you can imagine or visualize a line of energy being released from the center of your body deep into the earth.

Clearing - purification - cleansing the aura

The aura, the electromagnetic field that surrounds us, tends to be easily influenced by various factors. Some of the factors are internal, dependent on us, while others are external, environmental. The action of cleansing the aura, therefore, must not be neglected.

Energetic purification is especially important and significant to anyone who works on his extrasensory abilities, but actually there is no one who does not need it. Sensitive people must pay special attention to this activity as well as to grounding and protection, since without them they are liable to feel ill at ease constantly. Clearing is important mainly when we feel like "human sponges" - we absorb and pick up the energies of other people. On certain levels - especially when the sponge tends to be a person who is highly sensitive to energies - a state of emotional overload is liable to occur for no obvious reason after spending a lot of time in the company of people who are not emotionally balanced. In extreme situations, which are not rare, the person feels an irksome emotional imbalance after such encounters, to the point that he occasionally finds it difficult to distinguish which emotions are his, and which he simply picked up and absorbed from other people.

Holistic therapists who spend a lot of time in the presence of people that frequently suffer from a lack of emotional, physical, or spiritual balance are susceptible to a state of "energetic identification" in every therapeutic interaction. When working with people on releasing their emotions, strong emotions may emerge, and these emotions have unhealthy energetic frequencies that are emitted from the aura of the emotional body. A release of this kind occurs in many healing and alternative medicine techniques, in psychological treatments, and in various mental therapies. These energies are liable to reach the therapist and upset his equilibrium. This situation is extremely obvious when there is any identification - conscious or unconscious - between therapist and patient. Before the treatment, as well as before any extrasensory activity, the aura must be protected and strengthened. After the activity, it must be cleansed of all the non-positive energy that adhered to it.

Other people who must pay a great deal of attention to the matter of cleansing are those who spend a lot of time working with or in the vicinity of machines that emit radiation, such as computers, TV sets, microwaves, X-ray machines, and all the other the radiation-emitting electrical appliances.

As we said, everyone must practice cleansing techniques. However, energetically sensitive people must apply them on a daily basis in order to improve their feeling and purify themselves of non-positive energies.

There are different types of energetic purification. You might find a certain exercise more effective, and link up to it more easily. Having said that, it is advisable to practice the rest of the techniques a bit, so that you have a number of cleansing tools at your disposal in addition to the daily cleansing technique you have chosen. As you gain experience in the strengthening, protecting, and cleansing of the aura, you might find unique exercises that suit you perfectly and fit in with your daily routine.

Before I describe a number of well-known techniques, I will point out two simple cleansing methods that we use daily, without relating them to the cleansing of the aura: showering and washing hands. A cold shower is very effective for balancing the ionic state of the body, and has a soothing and liberating effect. In addition, it cleanses the electromagnetic field, but not always sufficiently. In order to reinforce the shower's effect on the aura, you must consciously direct your thoughts to the cleansing and purification of the aura while you are showering. Soap does not have a purifying effect on our electromagnetic field; on the contrary, it tends to block energy. Therefore, after cleaning yourself physically with soap and shampoo, stand under the running water for a few minutes and let it flow over your body. While doing so, it is advisable to shake your body a bit, relax your muscles, direct your thoughts to cleansing the aura, and pass your hands over the estimated perimeter of the electromagnetic field - at a distance of outstretched arms, similar to the brushing technique I will describe later.

Washing hands, too, with the conscious intention of cleansing and purifying the electromagnetic field and directing your thoughts to this aim, contributes significantly to the cleansing of the aura field. Usually, hand-washing is performed directly upon rising in the morning, before touching the body or any food. In addition to washing hands, cleansing must be performed during the day in every situation in which we come into contact with unwanted energies, or after being in an energetically impure place.

I recommend that you try each technique below a few times and select the one you prefer.

Ritual cleansing - the four elements

As we said, there are many cleansing methods, and as you get to know yourself and your energy field more deeply, you can invent a suitable one for yourself. Ritual cleansing according to the four elements - earth, water, air, and fire - is matched to the person according to the balance of the elements in him. The efficacy of the various techniques that derive from elemental cleansing depends on the strength or weakness of the various elements in the person's nature.

Earth: People with a weak earth element have a slight tendency toward levitating, sometimes toward slight physical weakness, pallor, intense mental activity as opposed to a lack of physical activity, and sometimes toward a high sensitivity to energies. People who lack the earth element are likely to find the grounding exercises in this book suitable for purification as well. Similarly, people with earth signs - Virgo, Taurus, and Capricorn - may find grounding an effective method of energetic cleansing.

Water: Purifiying with water is recommended for people whose water element is unbalanced. This can be expressed in a state of relatively frequent emotional imbalance, mood swings, and emotional instability. Cleansing with water is very suitable for people with water signs - Cancer, Scorpio, and Pisces. It is a good idea to focus on the feeling that the water is rinsing off the excess emotional energy. Energetic purification in seawater is also recommended. If you are not near water and feel that you are in need of cleansing, see yourself in your mind's eye standing under a turbulent waterfall, or bathing into a flowing stream. See how the water washes over your entire body, and feel its coolness and purity. Continue with this visualization for a few minutes.

Air: Purification with air is very suitable for people with air signs - Gemini, Libra, and Aquarius - especially at times of emotional confusion and a burden of non-supportive emotions. For them, the wind is an effective tool for dispelling excess emotional energies. This is a method of purification that is extremely simple, and can be applied in a number of ways: sitting opposite a fan, traveling in a car with the window open (not when you are driving) so that the wind blows against your face and chest, a fast bicycle-ride in the wind, running into the wind, and so on. When you do these actions, see the wind blowing all the unwanted energies away from you, and carrying you far away, purifying and aerating you. You can also sit opposite an open window and visualize in your mind's eye the wind blowing on and around you, as it purifies you and blows all the non-positive energies away.

Fire: People with fire signs - Aries, Leo, and Sagittarius - often find themselves attracted to fire and warm colors such as gold, red, yellow, and orange. Light and fire exercises are very suitable for them. In order to fill up with energy, these people are advised to do their filling up and protection with golden light. The combination of this process with the aura-cleansing process using the brushing technique is very effective. Similarly, they are advised to visualize themselves in their mind's eye surrounded by a glowing aura of golden light.

Although the tendency is to match the elemental cleansing to the members of the various signs according to the element that belongs to them, I have discovered that people sometimes find one of the other methods to be their appropriate way of purification. If you feel great when you are in water, and your natural instinct is to take a shower when you feel tired or agitated, or you especially revel in the wind blowing in your face, or feel a need to sit close to fire or to dig your toes into the sand at the shore, you can find the purifying method that is suitable for you by experimenting with the different elements. Of course, you can experiment with all the cleansing methods, all the while noting in your awareness notebook the "before" and "after" feelings, and in this way you can know which of the methods are most effective for you when you experience a particular energetic situation.

The brushing technique

This is a quick and easy purification technique that is excellent to apply after you have been in a place that you felt to be energetically unclean. Sometimes this feeling occurs after a hospital visit because of the energy of pain and sorrow that exists there and in various other institutions. It occurs in pubs where people fill their bodies with alcohol and try to barricade themselves emotionally against the experiences of life. You may feel it after being in a home where energies of quarrels and anger were present. You may feel it after you yourself were immersed in non-positive energies - energies of turbulence, worry, anger, or sorrow.

Stand with your body upright and comfortable. Shake your legs and arms slightly, release them, and relax your body. Take three deep, slow breaths. Direct your thoughts to cleansing your electromagnetic field of all unwanted energies. Using your palm or the back of your hand, begin to rub every part of your body vigorously with brushing movements. Start by running your fingers through your hair, shake it, spread it out, and stroke your whole hand over it, as if you were pulling and extracting all the unwanted energy from it. Shake your hands at your sides in order to get rid of the energy that adhered to them. Pass your palms gently over your face, with the direction of the movement being from the center of your face outward, as if you were "removing dust" from your face. Continue with a light brushing of your neck, from above (below your chin) downward (toward your shoulders). After a few movements, shake your hands and release the energies that adhered to them. Continue to the shoulders. Brush them with more vigorous motions, as if you were dusting off your clothing. If you suffer from a lot of tension in your shoulder region, use a bit of strength when you perform the brushing movements.

After you have cleansed your shoulders, go on to brush your arms. Start by brushing your left arm with your right hand. Brush the entire length of your arm with a strong, continuous, pulling motion to your fingertips and shake your right hand (which did the brushing). Repeat the action with the other hand and arm. When shaking your hands free of the energy you brushed, direct your thoughts to moving the unwanted energy downward, to the bowels of the earth. Afterwards, rub your chest and abdomen vigorously using downward brushing movements.

Then brush your back (as much as you can; in areas you cannot reach, direct your thoughts to cleanse them!), your buttocks, your inner and outer thighs and calves, with vigorous downward movements, until you reach your feet. There, you must direct your thoughts to shifting the non-positive energies downward, deep into the bowels of the earth.

After you have brushed your entire body with vigorous movements, shake your hands well, imagine in your mind's eye a jet of cold water washing them, and "cleanse" them in the purifying jet of water. Afterwards, with slow and gentle motions, and taking a slow and conscious breath, slowly move the palm of your hand at a distance of a few centimeters from your body, trying to feel the aura field. Start above your head, and slowly descend along both sides of your body, not forgetting the inner side of the arms and legs, from the left, the right, front, and back (wherever you cannot reach, imagine that you are moving the non-positive energy downward).

Finish next to your feet, and imagine that you are causing the non-positive energy to sink downward, deep into the bowels of the earth.

You can apply the brushing technique to other people, to animals, and to plants as well. Of course, it should be done gently, paying attention to their reactions and emotions. Always remember to shake your hands after brushing off the energy, and to direct the non-positive energy downward into the bowels of the earth. The technique is also very good when you feel exhausted, fatigued, and drained after being in an energetically unclean place, after a treatment, and after a lot of work at a computer.

Cleansing the aura by means of incense

This is an easy and effective way of cleansing the aura, and it is used mainly after administering a treatment, after a quarrel, argument, or a long, busy day, and when there you feel that non-positive energies have adhered to your aura. The cleansing is done with the help of a partner, who holds the stick of incense. After you do this cleansing with the help of a partner often, you may be able to do it by yourself.

For the cleansing, you can use any stick of natural and high-quality incense. (There are incense sticks that are scented with low-quality artificial perfumes that are used for purifying the air in toilets, walk-in closets, and so on - it is not advisable to use them.) The types of incense that are most highly recommended are sage, which is very strong and effective for purification, frankincense, and jasmine. However, any stick of high-quality, pleasant-smelling incense will do.

Stand erect, feet slightly apart, and close your eyes.

Make sure to take deep, slow, and comfortable abdominal breaths. Your partner holds the lit and smoking stick of incense and begins to walk around your body. There are many different ways of moving the incense around, but it should go in a right-to-left direction - clockwise. It is possible to start at the top, and move the incense stick clockwise around the head, at a distance of 20 to 60 centimeters from the body, and gradually descend, in a kind of spiral, to the feet, and then ascend again.

Another way is to start on the right side of the body and descend very slowly to the feet, and then go up the left side of the body, go down the right side again, and go up the left side once more. In this technique, intuition and emotion are very important, and if your partner feels that another slightly different method of moving the incense stick around is appropriate, it is worth trying. This technique is simple, quick, and extremely effective. After the cleansing, you frequently experience a feeling of relief and purification, a feeling of a burden being lifted off your shoulders, greater vitality, and a feeling of significant tranquillity.

Acorn

The acorn, the fruit of the oak tree, is very important as an amulet. The origin of this belief lies in the Druid culture, which maintained that the acorn brought good luck to the person who carried it, and it is obvious that this is linked to the acorn's being the seed of the sacred oak tree. This superstition is prevalent in the Mediterranean countries, where the oak is ubiquitous. The acorn links man with nature and protects him from the evil spirits of nature.

A custom that has survived to this day is to place an acorn or a string of acorns on the windowsill. Some people grind a dried acorn and sprinkle the powder in the house, mainly to protect the house and its occupants from fire or a bolt of lightning.

The acorn is a seed that takes a very long time to sprout, so it is a good idea for a person who encounters difficulties on the path to realizing his ambitions to take an acorn as an amulet. In this way, he will gain the perseverance, patience, and tolerance of the acorn.

The wheel of the year

At the beginning of this book, we encountered the great lunar cycles. In my opinion, those are the most important cycles of wicca, since they are personal and concern every living creature and Mother Earth in a "personal" manner. However, from the ceremonial point of view, much more is known about the festivals or "key points" in the solar cycle, which are connected to the sun and therefore also to the seasons.

We find eight major wicca festivals that together turn and ultimately create the wheel of the year. These festivals are called "sabbats."

In fact, the wicca sabbats go back to the directional division of the winds that is customary in eastern traditions. (Remember the I Ching or the Feng Shui principles - there are eight types of wind: south, southwest, west, northwest, north, northeast, east, southeast. The sabbats resemble the directions of these winds, except that they are sketched on the calendar.

The eight sabbats, or solar festivals, occur at intervals of about 45 days, and "close" the 365-day calendar in a complete cycle. They are seasonal festivals, linked mainly to the influence of the cosmic changes on Mother Earth. This is because of the fact that wicca is closely linked to nature and its phenomena and processes. The change of seasons reflects the cycle of changes in nature, which is essential to agrarian societies. However, we must not forget (as is emphasized in various myths) that these festivals also indicate the Shanti trinity of the goddess - the virgin, the mother, and the old woman, or the cycle of birth, fertility, and death.

The festivals that are determined according to the new and full moon - 12 or 13 during the solar year - are called "esbats," or lunar festivals. In addition to those, every day of the week has a different significance for the wicca practitioner. In sum, the wicca practitioner has about 20 central festivals for performing the ceremonies - more than enough to fill the entire year with practical wicca.

Sabbats

All Saints' Night - Samhain

Samhain, which is also called Halloween, All Saints' Night/ Day? and the Day of the Dead, falls on October 31. Samhain (pronounced "sow-enn") has become known as the "witches' New Year." Although it is mentioned here first, there is no practical importance to this, since it is located on a wheel that has neither "head" nor "tail." In fact, this festival is of secondary importance in the eight festivals of the sun.

For this festival, accessories such as red apples, spiral shapes, dry branches, dark mirrors (for making contact with the next world), and crystal balls are used. The dominant colors in this festival are brown and black. Today, the festival is used mainly for rituals connected with prophecy or predictions.

This festival is extremely important in the wicca calendar that was developed in agrarian society. This is the time following the grain harvest, and the farmers would estimate the number of livestock they could feed during the winter. The remaining cattle would be slaughtered, and that is why this festival is also linked to "the red harvest" - the festival during which many animals were slaughtered and their meat was preserved for the winter.

The festival marks the time when the souls of all those who died during the year go over to "the other side," and all the souls of those to be born during the coming year enter this world. The festivities are directed at those who died, especially those who died during the past year. Moreover, it is customary to mention the forefathers and to relate various myths. Because of the connection with the next world, this is the time of year in which "the curtain between the worlds is thinnest," and sorcery is extremely powerful and effective.

A widespread ceremony during Samhain is "the feast of the mute," so called because it is not customary to talk during the ceremony, since the dead also participate in the feast and do not utter a sound - they just eat. This feast is shared with those who have left the world. An extra plate is placed on the table for those who are no longer with us. I am sure that every reader will recall a similar custom linked to the dead in his or her culture. After the meal, the plate is taken out and placed on the threshold of the house.

The Samhain meal consists mainly of the last "produce" of the fields and trees before the winter and the harvest, as well as of many meat dishes.

In myths, this is the festival in which the goddess mourns her husband, the god, who has been killed, and awaits the imminent birth of his child, or for his return (as in the case of Tammuz). The festival therefore signals the death of the god, who sacrifices his life for the community.

The winter solstice - Yule

Yule, which is also called the winter solstice, falls on December 21. Yule is the day that became Christmas.

The main component is the evergreen tree, and beside it, everything connected to the sun - oranges, shiny crystals, gold, candles, and so on. The dominant colors are gold, white, red, green - but also black. The festival is exploited mainly for ceremonial festivities, or for treating health problems.

This is the time of year in which winter dominates the earth, so it is a time of leisure that is dedicated to the telling of legends and myths. It is the longest night, and wicca traditions include burning a log that was ignited before sunset and ensuring that it burns all night. "It is born with the setting sun, takes of its light, and guards its life until it appears once more, and then it (the log) dies and its ashes are collected on the good earth," as is written in an ancient Celtic text.

Yule trees are decorated anew every year (decorating an evergreen tree is a traditional pagan custom). The Yule meal includes many components that are considered "Christmas dishes," such as sweets and cookies, roasts and stews. After Yule, the members of the wicca groups customarily exchange gifts, and it goes on until "Twelfth Night," which is a Christian holiday known as "Little Christmas," which began in the Middle Ages and is celebrated 12 days after Christmas.

In myths, the goddess gives birth to the god of the sun during the longest night of the year, and witches and wizards celebrate the birth (or rebirth) of the god of the sun.

Imbolc

This festival, which is celebrated on February 1 or 2, is also called Candelmas or Imlich. Imbolc is a time when winter still resides on the earth, but spring is approaching. In agrarian societies, this is a turning point - it does not matter what state you were in during the winter; now a new season of sowing-growing-harvest is beginning. The lengthening of the days is noticeable, and the long, dark nights are coming to an end. This is also the coldest time of the year (in Europe, where these festivals were founded), so that survival during the winter is a serious test.

The accessories that are the "vestiges" of the winter include snowflake-shaped decorations, candles or light sources, onions and bulbs. The dominant colors are white or pale green. The festival is excellent for cleansing the aura and grounding, purification rites, healing, and candle spells.

The witches and wizards celebrate around a fire, a bonfire, or candles. In certain agrarian societies, this was the time when agricultural implements were passed through fire in order to bless them. Preparations are made for the planting season in the spring. The blacksmith's shop in which the agricultural implements are created and in which the link between fire, wind and iron is forged, serves as the focal point of the wicca rituals during this festival.

In the groups that I initiate, every participant brings a tool that goes through a ritual of passing through fire and blessing during this festival. Everyone brings the tool that is important to him.

In the myths, this is the time in which the goddess recuperated from the birth of the child, and the child lived and became stronger; in other words, he survived. Imbolc may also be a time of initiation and consecration. Some people see this time as a time of the renewal of the goddess as a virgin after the birth of her son (that is, the renewal of her virginity as a symbol of her purity).

The spring equinox - Oestarra

Oestarra falls on March 21, which is also known as the spring equinox, when day and night are equal in length. This is the source of the Christian Easter festival. This can be seen in the strong resemblance between the names and the characteristic customs. In principle, this is the time of the spring celebrations (or the coming spring), celebration of fertility, and the expectation of the season of growth. Even if the earth is still partially covered with snow, it is clear that the end of the winter is approaching. This is a day of equilibrium, when day and night are equal in length.

The accessories that are used in the rituals are spring flowers, eggs painted green, and various cakes. The dominant color is green. It is a good festival for fertility rites. It is a good time for new beginnings.

There are traditions that celebrate the change from the "dark" half of the year - the goddess's half - to the "light" half of the year - the god's half. It is celebrated with dishes made of fresh vegetables and plants that grow in the spring. During this festival, the goddess changes from an old woman to a virgin, and she is once more a young girl ready for growth (and nurtures the god of the sun who is growing rapidly during this season).

May Eve/Mayday - Beltane
Beltane is celebrated on May 1 or April 30. It is also known by the name, May Eve. Beltane is one of the important festivals in the wicca calendar. It is also called the fertility festival.

The accessories used during this festival are blooming flowers, colored ribbons, chaplets and crowns of leaves and flowers, and poles decorated with flowers, leaves, and fruit. The dominant colors are green, white, and pink. It is an excellent festival for rituals of love and sex, and for everything to do with fertility.

In myths, the goddess and the god reach sexual maturity and are aware of their sexuality. The goddess changes from a virgin to a mother. This is the springtime, the time for sowing and planting, and the mating period for animals. In agrarian societies, it was customary to bless the fields, and couples would go out to the fields and make love in the bosom of nature in order to help renew the fertility of the earth symbolically.

Witches and wizards celebrate with a feast of spring vegetables. Fresh flowers are brought in order to celebrate the new season of blossoming.

Sometimes a "May-queen" and a "May-king" are appointed, and they become the representatives of the goddess and the god for a day. They serve as spiritual advisors to the members of the group. Only people who have gone through initiation can be appointed queen or king. In different traditions, there is a custom of exchanging gifts of May baskets along with wishes for fertility and a prosperous summer.

Beltane is a happy festival. Spring is already here and summer is coming. It is also the season for the festivals that take place outdoors in nature.

Midsummer

Midsummer, or the longest day of the year, is celebrated on June 21. During this period, the first fruits begin to appear on the trees. Life is easy and good, there is food, and the cold weather is disappearing. The days are warm and long. In myths, this is the time in which the goddess is impregnated by the god, her belly swells, and new life is created in her vicinity. In agrarian societies, this is the time between sowing and reaping - the time in which Mother Earth "swells."

The accessories used in the rituals include pink roses, oak leaves, and various symbols connected with the sun. The dominant colors are red and green. This is a good festival for personal spells, as well as for those that are done for the sake of society and the universe as a whole.

This time is suitable for festivals. Witches and wizards

celebrate with feasts of fruit and vegetables. Even though it is the longest day of the year, it carries with it the awareness that from now on, the days will get shorter, and the winter will ultimately arrive. This is the time of the goddess as a mother, and she is at the peak of her glory.

Lammas

Lammas (also called Lughnasadh) is celebrated on August 1. This festival celebrates the first fruits of the harvest, and a big feast is part of the sacred ritual. This is the celebration of the first harvest. The summer fruits are ripening and the gardens are full of vegetables. The days are becoming shorter, and people are aware of the approach of the winter. A lot of breads and cakes are backed.

The accessories that are used are grains (sheaves, for instance), cookies (including cookies shaped like people or animals), and fresh breads. The dominant color is bright orange. This is a suitable time for breaking up (relationships), for spiritual enlightenment and initiation (including holding a ceremony for admission into a wicca group).

In myths, some people see this time as the time when the god dies, sacrificing himself in order to enable the community to exist. (The goddess is already carrying a child in her womb, and so there is a continuation to the family.)

The autumn equinox - Mabon

Mabon, which falls on September 21, is also known as the day in autumn in which day and night are of equal length. This is the other day of equilibrium, in which the length of the day and the night are equal. It can symbolize the transition from the period of the god, or the period of light of the year, to the period of the goddess, or the period of dark of the year. Sometimes the death of the god is celebrated at this time.

In myths, this is the death of the god as voluntary sacrifice - the god is at the height of his power and forfeits his life for the wellbeing of the people.

The accessories that are customary for this festival are apples, autumn leaves, and acorns. The dominant colors are orange, brown, gold, and red. This festival is suitable for reinforcing mental powers.

The witches and wizards celebrate this festival with a feast of cereals, fruit and vegetables - the first apples are extremely important.

Unicorn

The unicorn is a mysterious creature that features in almost every known culture. According to the belief, the unicorn disappeared from the world after it was expelled from Noah's ark. But can anyone say for sure where a unicorn that has not yet become extinct will suddenly pop up?

The unicorn resembles a horse, but what makes it special is the single, straight horn in the center of its forehead. Properties of purity and sanctity are attributed to the unicorn, and it symbolizes virginity, fidelity, and "human" warmth.

Only a virgin can touch a unicorn, and this is why the sign of the Zodiac for Virgo often depicts a young girl beside a unicorn, so that everyone will understand that she is a virgin. A piece of jewelry in the shape of a unicorn can symbolize the same thing.

The unicorn's horn, which is white, black, and red, can warn of danger, purify tainted water, and cure illnesses - all this just by a mere touch. Powdered unicorn's horn is an important ingredient in any magic potion, and it is especially effective for preparing a potion that makes the person invisible.

A pinch of powdered unicorn's horn restores men's virility, and is considered to be the ultimate aphrodisiac... and this is the reason why the rhinoceros, for instance, is becoming extinct. Its single horn is a substitute for the unicorn's horn!

The objects used in wicca

When you begin to take part in actual wicca rituals, you will immediately notice that an extremely wide range of tools and objects is used. Since every wicca group can choose the objects it uses, we find a large selection of objects that are used in wicca (also called consecrated objects). For example, I use the symbols of the Tarot cards - the sword (transformed into a dagger in wicca), the cup, the pentagram, and the wand. As you no doubt know, those are the four symbols of the Tarot arcanas.

The dagger

The most conspicuous accessory of every participant in wicca rituals is the dagger - a consecrated knife that is used to "separate this from that" and to direct enchanted energies. The most handsome dagger is the one that is called "the witches' dagger" - a dagger with a black handle about 10 cm in length and a two-edged blade about 15 cm in length. Witches and wizards prefer the handle to be made of a natural substance such as wood, leather, or bone.

For witches and wizards, it is a sacred tool. It is important to mention that this dagger is never used as a weapon, nor is it used to slaughter or harm animals or plants.

This dagger is also considered to be personal. When a person touches someone else's dagger without permission, it is considered to be an invasion of defined personal space.

The dagger is used to attract or direct energies and for marking the area used as a circle.

The dagger symbolizes the element of fire as well as reason, which cuts away everything that is not the truth, distinguishing between truth and falsehood.

Some witches and wizards are not prepared to carry a dagger (since it is, after all, a weapon), so they exchange it for a "symbolic" dagger - the index finger and middle finger of the left hand, close together and erect. This symbolic dagger can be a substitute for the witches' dagger.

The cup

The cup is used as a container for holy water, wine, or other beverage (for example, fermented apple juice), and it symbolizes the womb. Wicca focuses on nature, which is linked to Mother Earth, and on the principle of fertility, and the wine in the cup is an expression of this.

The cup symbolizes the element of water, which is connected to the womb and the female element.

The pentagram

The pentagram (which appears on the coin in Tarot cards) symbolizes the element of earth. The pentagram generally appears on a disk or a plate as a diagram of a five-pointed star. The pentagram is sometimes made of wax (and is not etched). In this form, it can be "burned in fire" and eliminated, thus canceling the (black) magic in it. However, the pentagram is generally etched in wood, metal, stone, or any other solid substance.

The pentagram is used to ground the energies.

The wand

The wand is actually a stick, generally about 40 cm in length, used to direct enchanted energies (though differently than with the dagger). Wands can be wooden sticks or an artistic creation combining crystals and decorations.

The wand represents the element of air.

Other objects I use are:

A bowl of water
A bowl that contains water. The water is used for protection and purification.

A bowl of salt
A small bowl that contains salt. The salt is used for protection and purification.

Candles
Light is considered to be the expression of divine energy, and candles are very important in wicca (as in many other religions). The candle is a symbol of enlightenment.

The color of the candles is very significant, and every color serves a different purpose in wicca.

White candles are the most useful ones. They are used in prayers and in initiation ceremonies. They symbolize pure light, cleanliness, and enlightenment.

A black candle can occasionally symbolize the goddess (together with a white candle that symbolizes the god).

Red or pink candles are used in rituals to solicit love, to send love, or to make contact with a beloved person who is far away. (Red candles stress physical passions; pink candles stress gentle love, softness and innocence.)

Green candles are used in rituals for Mother Earth and the animals and plants it contains. They are also used in rituals soliciting abundance and prosperity.

Brown candles are used when there is a need for a stabilizing effect. They are also used in rituals for healing Mother Earth and for linking up to it.

Blue candles are used in rituals for releasing self-expression and increasing creativity.

Purple candles are used for prayers and meditation whose objective is to reinforce extrasensory abilities. They can also be used for soothsaying.

Yellow candles are used for increasing joy, happiness, good fortune, and for requests for equilibrium.

Orange candles are used in rituals and prayers for increasing motivation and self-confidence.

Magenta candles are used for fortifying healing powers.

Candle (in the field of superstitions)

The candle is a very important factor in the field of superstitions. Its main function is to bring light into places where human beings go... and to dispel the darkness, of course. Darkness is linked to the evil eye, and light to good luck. Therefore, the burning candle is a tried, tested, and accepted means of getting rid of the evil eye.

There are many superstitions linked to it. Some people light candles around a dead body (generally 12 candles) in order to create a ring of light. Others light three candles (in parallel to the Holy Trinity) for the same purpose.

The candle, especially the candle that is found in holy places - churches or the graves of saints - is important for making potions and amulets. There is a great deal of belief in the power of a "holy" candle to help a barren woman give birth, or to strengthen a man's virility... and there is no doubt that there is an inextricable link between the shape of the candle and the male member.

A burning candle gives off light, and this light is very significant. Blue light emanating from the candle always attests to good luck, for instance.

When a candle goes out during a religious ritual, it is irrefutable proof that the evil eye is in the vicinity, and that the forces of evil are invading the candle's realm!

Candles, which were made principally out of beeswax in the past, were thought to be holy because of the belief that bees originated in the Garden of Eden. This is the source of the belief that chewing the remains of holy candles fortifies the health and contributes to the curing of serious illnesses.

Candles can serve as voodoo dolls when necessary. Sticking pins in the candle while pronouncing the name of the person's sweetheart will strengthen the bond of love. The pin must be stuck in the candle, which is then lit and allowed to burn down. The scorched pins must be carried as an amulet of love.

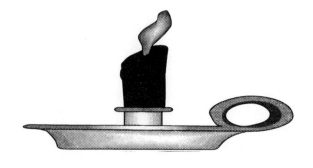

Plants, herbs, and incense

Like many of my friends, I make a great deal of use of plants and herbs (and incense), which are the symbol of vitality and life. Witches and wizards make extensive and varied use of the plant world. Potions, infusions, ointments, incense, decorations, and so on can be prepared from the plants. The knowledge of plants and herbs, and the ability to know their uses, as well as the ability to distinguish between poisonous and beneficial plants, are the professional tools of wicca. Here is a long list of plants and their uses, in alphabetical order:

Acacia - Since the acacia has both white and red flowers, it serves as a symbol of life and death, or death and rebirth. The thorns of the acacia represent the horns of the crescent moon and can be used in lunar rituals. The acacia tree is also a solar tree. It is sometimes used in initiation ceremonies (the person must know how to die in order to live again in the eternal world).

Almond - used as a symbol of reinforcing feminine power.

Aloe - used for attracting energies of honesty and wisdom.

Apple - used widely in love rituals as a symbol of love, fertility, and marriage. The peel can be used in various wicca ceremonies. It also symbolizes unity as well as "art" (that is, the quest for wisdom). In Celtic witchcraft traditions, the apple is considered to possess powerful properties of (mainly black) magic and witchcraft, and it is also considered to be a fruit of the next world. Halloween is sometimes called the festival of the apple, and the apple plays the leading role in the festive meals as a symbol of the death of the old year. The flowers of the apple tree are used to adorn the bride in the joining hands ceremony.

Arum lily - serves as a symbol of peace, purity, and fertility of the goddess of the earth. It is a symbol of the renewed virginity of the goddess, and of renewal in general. It represents the feminine principle.

Aster - a plant and flower that symbolize love.

Bamboo - used for strength in old age.

Barley - occasionally used in ritual feasts as a symbol of new life after death, the god's return to life, and the revival of the spring and its return to the earth. It is linked to the white goddess. Moreover, barley is a species of grain.

Basil - used at funerals and in rites for the dead.

Bean - has a place of honor in witchcraft. It symbolizes the power of the witchcraft itself, as well as immortality.

Beech - a symbol of prosperity and soothsaying.

Black coral - used for releasing repressed emotions and for protection against negative energies.

Camelia - used in witchcraft to attract stability, health, beauty and mental and physical strength.

Cedar - a symbol of power, nobility, and clean hands.

Cherry - symbolizes the person who comes naked into the world, with no property, and returns to the earth in the same way - naked.

Chestnut - used against temptation. Safeguards modesty and purity.

Citron - symbolizes love.

Clover - used as a symbol of stimulating celestial properties, and symbolizes the three aspects of life - body, mind, and spirit.

Coral - symbolizes communal and shared life. Considered the goddess-mother tree, and used for expressing lunar energies as symbolizing the fertility of water.

Corn - used as a symbol of abundance and fertility and is linked to the sun. It is also considered to be a species of grain. It symbolizes the idea of multiplying and growth. The cob can be used as a symbol of unity or inspiring unity among the members of the group - many individuals who create one whole. Many wicca groups dry corn cobs together, and separate the kernels from the cob in a ceremony that is meant to join the members of the group to one another.

Cyclamen - used in ceremonies as a symbol of purity and youth.

Cypress - linked to the sun and the moon alike, to the god and the goddess. The branches of the cypress were used in rites of passage to the next world as well as in burial rites.

Daisy - a flower that symbolizes solar power, innocence, and purity.

Date - used in rituals and feasts as a symbol of abundance and fertility.

Elm - used to attract respect and status.

Fennel - a plant that is widely used in witchcraft. A symbol of fire. The stem of the fennel is used as a staff in rituals connected with Mother Earth. There are wicca communities that are in the habit of holding "duels" with fennel stems in cases of conflicts between members of the group.

Fig - an important symbol in ritual feasts: life, fertility, prosperity, and peace. The fruit represents feminine power, and the leaves represent masculine power. Because of the shape of its fruit, which resembles both the female breasts and the gaping vagina, the fig tree is identified with femininity and fertility. Some people see the fig tree as the tree of life (the protector of paradise).

Fir - symbolizes audacity, honesty, and patience.

Gardenia - used to attract feminine favors.

Garlic - a plant that protects against the evil eye and negative spells.

Grain - different types of grains are used in ceremonies and in ritual feasts as a sign of the fertility of the earth and of abundance. Grains are linked to the sun, which permits growth. Grain and new wine together (bread and wine, sometimes in combination with salt) symbolize nature that permits life. Grains are widespread in rites of passage to the next world.

Grapes - used in feasts and rituals as a symbol of fertility and abundance for what comes from nature (mother earth).

Grapevine - used as an extremely powerful symbol of life and fertility.

Hyacinth - symbolizes wisdom and caution. Symbol of resurrection in the spring.

Hyssop - a plant with extremely powerful properties of purification. Also symbolizes humility and innocence.

Iris - used for attracting light and hope. Can appear in rites of passage to the next world, as a companion of the dead person's soul.

Ivy - a symbol of fidelity and friendship. Characterizes feminine power.

Jasmine - used mainly to attract love and as a symbol of femininity.

Juniper - The juniper plant is considered to be the preserve of pagan spirits and fairies, sometimes even the entrance gate to the other world. It is used for extrasensory protection. In rites of passage to the next world, juniper leaves are burned in order to banish evil spirits.

Laurel (bay) - a symbol of victory, peace, immortality and eternity. Laurel leaves are used for stimulating motivation.

Lemon - used in joining and partnership ceremonies (joining hands), as a symbol of fidelity and love... but is also used in separation and detachment ceremonies.

Lettuce - used in ritual feasts as a symbol of fertility.

Lotus - a plant that is used for attracting love and as a symbol of love. Both lunar and solar, it symbolizes both god and goddess, life and death. It joins the forces of the sun (fire) and the moon (water). It symbolizes renewal, immorality, fertility, and the creation of perfect beauty. In wicca, many people consider the lotus a symbol of perfection because its fruit and flowers create the shape of a circle. It is an important mystical symbol.

Mandrake - a symbol of the great mother, who gives life. It is a plant of witchcraft. Many properties have been attributed to it because its root resembles the human form. There is a belief that whoever uproots the mandrake from the earth is liable to die, and for this reason, it was customary to tie a dog to the plant in order to uproot it. Mandrakes are effective for fertility, and therefore the plant is used for this purpose, as well as for increasing male virility.

Marigold - used in a spell for creating or attracting fidelity between the members of a couple.

Mistletoe - a central plant in witchcraft traditions that derive from Druid sources. Mistletoe is a parasite that grows on the oak tree and symbolizes the essence of life, and it is the symbol of immortality. Since it is neither tree nor bush, it symbolizes the indefinable, and therefore freedom from limitations, so that anyone who stands under the mistletoe is free of limitations. Mistletoe is the "golden plant" of the Druids and represents the consecrated female principle (the oak is the male principle). The Druids used it in their fertility rites. It symbolizes new life and rebirth on the shortest day of the year. There is a belief that mistletoe is created from lightning that strikes the branches of the oak tree, and this belief increases its magic powers.

Mulberry - The mulberry has a trio of colors in its ripening stages - white, red, and black. It symbolizes the three initiation stages, as well as the three stages in human life: white - the pure, innocent child; red - the active age; black - old age and death. Some people attribute to the mulberry magical powers that combat the forces of darkness.

Myrtle -used in rituals to attract love. It is considered to be an enchanted plant that brings merriment, calmness, and joy.

Myrrh - an incense plant that is wonderful for purifying and cleansing consecrated ground and for reinforcing and purifying spiritual energies.

Nut - used for occult wisdom, fertility, and longevity.

Oak - symbolizes power, protection, courage, endurance, and stability. The oak is consecrated to Mother Earth, and in the Celtic tradition is considered to be a holy tree. In the Druid tradition, it is a consecrated tree, the male principle, together with the white mistletoe that grows on it and symbolizes the female principle.

Olive - used in ceremonies as a symbol of peace, immortality, marriage, fertility, and abundance. The olive leaf symbolizes the renewal of life.

Onion - can be used in ceremonies and feasts as a symbol of peeling away mental layers in order to reach inner truth.

Orange - the blooming of the orange tree serves as a symbol of fertility. The fruit is used to bring good fortune or to attract pure love.

Orchid - used for attracting love and as a symbol of love. It symbolizes feminine energies, refinement and charm.

Palm - a symbol of the sun's powers, fertility, and victory.

Pansy - used for recalling forgotten things and for reinforcing meditative and thinking abilities.

Parsley - a mystical plant. Represents the female principle.

Peach - a fruit that is used as a symbol of spring, youth, marriage.

Pear - used as a symbol of hope and good health, passion and fertility.

Pine - Since it is an evergreen tree, it is used as a symbol of immortality.

Pineapple - a fruit that is a symbol of fertility and is used in fertility rites.

Pinecone - a symbol of fertility and good fortune.

Pink coral -used for inspiring love and fortifying it.

Plane - used for reinforcing learning abilities and powers.

Plum - used in wicca spells for attracting independence, fidelity, and a lack of dependence.

Pomegranate - used in the feasts of wicca groups in order to symbolize the unity of the group as a whole, despite the fact that many individuals who are different than one another belong to the group. It is a symbol of the unity of the universe, of eternal life, of fertility, and of abundance.

Poplar - the leaves of the poplar come in different shades of green. For this reason it symbolizes the tree of life: light green on the water side - symbolizes the moon, and dark green on the fire side - symbolizes the sun.

Poppy - used as a symbol of the great mother. It symbolizes the night and is consecrated to the moon. It also serves as a symbol of fertility.

Pumpkin - used in rituals and white magic as a symbol of the link between the two worlds, the upper world and the lower world - day vs. night, life vs. death, disgrace vs. exaltation, sadness vs. happiness. It symbolizes the universe, the joining of the god and the goddess. In certain traditions, the pumpkin represents the female womb and breasts, and is therefore a symbol of nutrition.

Red coral -used for protection against spells and the evil eye.

Red rose - one of the most popular flowers in witchcraft for attracting love. It symbolizes beauty, grace, sensuality and passion, spring and youth - but also the mystery of life, the unknown.

Rice - considered to be food from a divine source. Symbol of plenty and divine provision, of eternal life, happiness and fertility. For this reason, it is thrown it on the bride at a wedding.

Rosemary - linked with the past - devotion to a certain memory, an incense plant in memorial ceremonies for those who have left this world. It is also used as a cleansing and purifying incense and as a means of raising ancient memories.

Strawberry - used as a symbol of fertility and sexuality.

Sycamore - The fruit of the tree serves as a symbol for the mother of the goddess, of renewal, nutrition, fertility, and love.

Tulip - used for attracting love or revealing love, as a symbol of perfect love.

Verbena - a plant for witchcraft, especially in the traditions that draw upon the Celtic tradition. It is also used for protection against spells and incantations.

Violet - used to attract modesty.

White rose - symbolizes enchantment and spiritual revelation. It is used in rites of passage to the next world as a symbol of renewed resurrection. A red and white rose serves as a symbol of the unity of opposites, or of fire and water.

Willow - an enchanted tree consecrated to the goddess of the moon. The weeping willow symbolizes lamentation, and is widespread in rites of passage to the next world. It symbolizes the strength in weakness, since it bends under the onslaught of fierce winds and straightens up afterwards.

Yarrow - considered to be a plant that is suitable for countering spells. It is used for preparing Chinese I Ching sticks for predicting the future.

Salt

Since time immemorial, amazing properties and superstitions have been attributed to salt. Salt is a crystalline substance that is produced as if by magic in water... and disappears in water. Salt is a pure product - that is, it does not contain any additional substances - that is white in color, and for this reason is considered to be "sacred." We must remember that in days of yore, salt was extremely valuable, expensive, and indispensable to human life. Salt was so expensive that in many countries, gathering and mining salt was the monopoly of the king or ruler.

Salt has good and bad properties.

The first superstition states that salt protects the person against the devil. This is why, when salt is spilled, it is a sign that the devil is in the vicinity, and the person's guardian angel caused him to spill the salt. Since the guardian angel is stationed behind the person's right shoulder, and the devil is behind his left shoulder, he must immediately take a pinch of the salt and throw it over his left shoulder in order to blind the devil!

However, spilled salt also foretells an imminent quarrel between the members of a couple, perhaps as a result of the fact that in the past, salt was very expensive. "A quarrel with a husband always starts with spilled salt!"

Spilled salt is not only the sign of a quarrel, but also foretells days of sadness. In North America, it is believed that salt predicts sadness... since many tears are needed to "rinse out" the salt. For this reason, it is customary to pour salt onto fire, or onto a range - in order to "dry up" the tears of sadness. Obviously, the fact that tears are salty is connected to this superstition.

When salt is sprinkled on the threshold of the home, the devil and his henchmen cannot get in. (In fact, when salt or ash is sprinkled on the floor, the devil won't come because he is afraid of leaving tracks.)

In order to greet an important or beloved guest, he is received with a gift in the form of bread and salt, or by placing a pinch of salt in his right hand.

If a pinch of salt is placed on a baby's tongue, he will have a long, happy, and healthy life.

Incidentally, salt was used as currency in the past, both in trade, and especially as soldiers' salaries. In fact, the word "salary" comes from "sal", the Latin word for "salt." This in fact means that "he is worth his salt."

There is a belief that salt provides immunity against poisons. This belief stems from the custom of former rulers, who would take a pinch of poison with their food in order to fortify their immunity against genuine poisoning. They mixed the poison with salt. This is the origin of the expression, "A pinch of salt a day prevents a change of ruler."

The expression, "salt of the earth," describes the cream of humanity. A Muslim proverb states that "salt was spilled between us," meaning that a covenant was sworn between people. In the East, salt is still a purifying and sanctifying substance. Salt is sprinkled in the Sumo wrestling ring before every match in order to purify it of the evil eye.

In Christianity, there is a belief that a person who spills salt is treacherous. Judas Iscariot, the man who betrayed Jesus and turned him in, is described as sitting at the Last Supper with a mound of salt on the table before him.

Linking up with animals

In the most ancient days,
When animals and humans too were on the earth,
A man could become an animal if he wanted
And an animal could become a man.
Sometimes they were humans
And sometimes animals
And there was no difference
They all spoke the same language.
                    (from a Native American poem)

Wicca is closely linked to the animal world - our relatives that live on Mother Earth - on her land, in her waters, in her air, and deep within her earth. Wicca helps us link up to our animal of strength, and we have to learn from them what they transmit to us.

We can learn a great deal from animals, whether by observing them - the physical animal - or by using them as a "pipeline" to transmit messages. The totem animal, which we will try to get to know in the next exercise, helps us with our spiritual development. Animals that we encounter by chance may also be a sign or teach us something. More than once, I have asked the universe a question and an animal that is rarely found in the region where I live enters my house. By channeling with an animal, or by recognizing the message or insight represented by the animal, I received an answer to my question. People who are very in touch with nature and Mother Earth are inclined to receive many messages in this manner, as are people who work to preserve the environment. It would seem that nature "rewards" them with signs and symbols in the form of the animals that cross their paths. Incidentally, the animal does not have to appear physically in front of you: for instance, you might pass a store window or billboard upon which a picture of an animal appears; the insight that it represents will help you at that moment; or you turn on the TV and see the animal whose insight you are waiting for). Channeling with animals is easy and natural; you just have to open your mind to the idea that animals can channel with us in exactly the same way that we, human beings, channel with one another, and channel well telepathically.

Channeling (Linking up) with an animal via observation

This apparently simple meditation is one of the most ancient forms of observation (meditation). Many of the ancient philosophers, priests, shamans, and spiritual teachers acquired knowledge by means of this observation. There is no need to set a time limit for the meditation, since this may vary from person to person, from one object of observation to another, and mainly from a beginning meditative exercise to the following exercises. You have almost certainly performed this meditation in the past without calling it "meditation," but rather curious observation. Children, like many ancient tribal members, are gifted with an inner trigger to perform this meditation in certain conditions, and they can persist with it for a long time. It is natural and simple for them, except in cases in which the parents instill a fear of animals in them from infancy. As parents, it is important to support this natural activity, and not stop it or create an artificial barrier between the child and nature - a barrier that stems from the parents' own fears. This ancient meditation symbolizes our link with the animal world, a link in which there is no separation, but rather connection and a single whole. In its upper layers, which are reached - after practicing various meditations extensively - as a result of a deep and natural link with the natural world, and as a result of deep spiritual openness, the meditation leads to a feeling of perfect unity with the object of observation. This means being able to feel its feelings, and understanding the way it perceives, its insights, and often even its language.

Animals and plants have a clear and obvious language. The legends about King Solomon and St. Francis of Assisi state that they could understand the language of animals and plants. These claims are not the product of a fertile imagination, nor are they characteristic of only those figures. Every person has this ability, but he has to cross the conceptual barrier that says that the nature of animals and plants is separate and different from that of human beings. When the person crosses this conceptual barrier, he feels a deep love for nature, various fears regarding nature and its creatures disappear, he is sensitive and caring toward nature, and he eschews any action that can damage it, in the same way as he avoids hurting people.

When we set about establishing communication with animals and plants, we must remember that just as various tribes and peoples have different languages, so it is with animals. Their language is not composed of words, but rather of gestures, movements, looks, unique sounds, and telepathic, extrasensory communication. Plants, too, have a unique language. In deep layers, when the person can "hear" his soul, and he channels with it and knows it, he can reach the stage of "hearing" animals' souls, and may even grasp their message via his extrasensory auditory sense (the fine sense of hearing) as actual words. These wonderful experiences of communication with animals and plants are not the privilege of a few exceptional people only, but rather result from a deep love of nature, from the ability to understand that we and everything around us are one, and from spiritual work and the expansion of our awareness. Moreover, many people are granted these abilities as a gift when they show profound respect, appreciation, and love for nature, and are sensitive to Mother Earth and her children, the plants and animals. In cases like these, they get to feel nature's love for them in a unique way. Nature communicates with them through the channel that they themselves have established with their very sensitivity, concern, and appreciation for it and its creatures. This is an astounding and moving love, which is expressed in many different ways - all of which fill these people with wonder and joy.

Meditation with animals

The essence of this meditation is observing an animal you have chosen, or that will choose you, at a particular moment.

It is a good idea to perform the initial meditation, before you have become accustomed to the feeling, in a place that is as quiet as possible for you and the animal. It should be a tranquil place, preferably in natural surroundings. Sit comfortably at a distance from which you can observe the animal. This animal may be an ant, a beetle, or any other insect, a dove, a cat, a dog, and so on. However, you should be able to look into its eyes, and it should be able to look into your eyes. Moreover, at least at the beginning, it should be an animal that you like or admire from the outset, and that will stay in your line of vision long enough time for you to observe it profoundly. Animals such as horses, cows, sheep, cats, or dogs (yes, your own dog is great for meditation!) are excellent options for the initial meditation.

Perform the meditation with openness and calmness, without expectations, prejudices, or wishes. When you do the meditation the first few times, and the link with nature is still not familiar or immediate, you should do it sitting or standing at some distance from the animal. Having said that, the meditation itself - the observation and the link-up - may also happen tangibly when you are involved in some kind of activity with the animal - touching, playing, stroking, feeding, and so on.

Look at the animal. Look at its unique shape. Look into its eyes as far as possible. Look at its body, concentrating totally on the object of observation. At this moment, only you and the object of observation exist. Look at the structure of its body - its muscles, its bones, its movements - and do so without using your mental layer. In other words, forget about the explanations and chapters on animal behavior that you remember from textbooks; do not relate to them. Look at the unique expressions of the animal. Let your observation of the animal evoke new insights in you. Look at the animal with appreciation, and while you are looking at it, project your awareness to it. The observation itself is the projection of awareness. Feel the connection between you until you can just about feel the animal's feelings - its unique steps, its unique body movement, its expressions, the feelings that it experiences when it is involved in certain activities. Notice every single detail about its body, concentrate totally on your object of observation, and allow yourself to forget yourself while doing so. Devote as much time as you deem necessary to the observation. At the end of it, thank the animal for its part in the experience and for the gifts it gave you, and wish it health, happiness, and self-fulfillment.

The range of insights and feelings evoked during the meditation is broad and unique. Moreover, it also depends on the state of balance of the chakras and on the stimulation of the third eye center, and, as we said before, on the ability to let the self link up completely to the object of observation. In addition to the insights we receive during meditation, the meditation helps us restore our natural reactive and healing abilities as an inseparable part of nature, and causes tremendous vitality to flow into our entire body.

People with a powerful extrasensory visual ability, who tend to see what they do during meditation with their inner eye, who often see clear dreams, or who are able to see content from the imagination in their mind's eye, can perform this meditation without the animal being present. For that, you should lie or sit comfortably, and enter a deep meditative state. In the meditation for observing animals using this technique, the possibilities for observing various animals are broader, since they do not depend on time or place, and you can summon any animal you like to it. You can also meditate without calling on any particular animal, but just let it appear. The animal that appears opposite your eyes may teach you a number of important insights. If the sight of this animal makes you feel somewhat uneasy or frightened, this is the time to make peace with it and remember that you are part of everything that exists, and the separation between the bodies is an illusion that belongs to this world only. Moreover, by meditating in this way (when the person can see the animal clearly in his mind's eye), the illusions stemming from the material world that are attributed to animals are extremely tenuous. This means that it is possible to listen to the animal and channel with it very easily without the limitations that people's perceptions tend to attribute to the animal world. If you hear the animal speaking during the meditation, or you feel as if it wants to talk to you, you can ask it a question. Animals have the ability to teach us many profound things, reveal secrets, instruct, and serve as messengers between us and the source. Various types of birds, especially the dove and the hawk, are excellent messengers, and we can ask them to relay our wishes to the source so that they can be fulfilled.

Your animal of strength - the totem animal

The concept of an animal of strength, or a totem animal, is widespread in many cultures. In the Jewish culture, there are examples of the use of animals as symbols of a personality or behavior type. Some of the pennants of the tribes of Israel bore pictures of the animal that represented the tribe. The most famous is the Lion of Judah. The writings of one of the sages, in which he suggested that it is preferable to be a lion's tail rather than a fox's head, describes the way in which our animal of strength is supposed to help us. In the Native American culture, every tribe, clan, and nuclear family had a totem. Today, too, in various organizations and companies, animals are used as symbols that represent the group that participates in a particular type of activity, mainly in the USA (such as the "Lions" organization, "The Generous and Protected Order of the Antelope", etc.). Sports teams also adopt totem animals, such as the Chicago Bulls. Christianity adopted two "totem" animals - the lamb, which symbolizes Jesus, and the fish.

As we said, in Judaism, too, every animal represents a particular kind of energy. The fish is a symbol of fertility, the lion is the symbol of power and strength, the deer is a symbol of speed, and so on.

The second type of totem animal is the personal and individual one. These animals are energies, and, according to certain beliefs, spirits that protect and guide us in life. It is interesting that to this day, many parents give their children some kind of fluffy animal - a bear, for instance - to make it easier to fall asleep and help them feel protected.

They are not aware of it, generally speaking, but this is also a totem animal.

The signs of the Zodiac also contain animals that attest more than once to the energy that influences the person's life.

Frequently, we unconsciously identify the totem animal of a particular person. We look at him, and he seems to "remind" us of a certain animal. We also use animal descriptions to describe various people.

Animals hold a place of honor among the shamans. The first task of the future shaman is to learn to travel in other worlds and dimensions and discover his own totem animal, his animal of strength. This knowledge is necessary for starting the young shaman's protracted learning process.

Personal animals of strength are generally the reflection of the self, and also represent qualities needed in this world, which are often hidden, concealed, and not yet expressed. Sometimes, people feel somewhat disappointed when they discover that their animal of strength is a "small" animal that seems to lack strength, such as a rabbit or a mouse. This error derives from a lack of understanding that the spirit of the animals, or their energies, is neither "small" nor "big" - it is not limited to the boundaries of this world and the physical reality and size of the animal, or to its strength in the physical world. None of those factors is relevant. Whether your animal of strength is "big" or "small," you will quickly discover that in time of need, it will help you exactly to the extent that you need help.

According to the Native American tradition, the personal totem animal, in contrast to family, clan, or tribal totem animals, may change several times during the person's lifetime, according to his specific needs. At times when you feel weak, exhausted, and depressed, your totem animal is far away from you, and you have to bring it back or find a new one.

We all have a totem animal - an animal of strength, energy that is represented by a certain animal - that is linked to us and protects us. Many animals of strength serve as our guards and protectors, and exist in other dimensions. Certain animals were with us in previous lives, but they may have had a different physical form. Occasionally, a particular animal of strength of ours may appear in our lives in a different form and establish physical contact with us by coming into the world as a cat, a dog, and so on.

In this chapter, I will present a number of ways for discovering personal animals of strength. When you go on the journey to discover your animal of strength, it is almost certain that forces, or certain energies (as we said, according to the Native American tradition, those are the spirits of the animal; I personally prefer to define them as the energy of the animal), will introduce themselves as your animal of strength. If you already know and are familiar with your animal of strength, the animal you meet on your journey will bless you and grant you additional power.

According to the Native American tradition, all birds and mammals are positive totem animals. Any positive totem animal can be your animal of strength. However, not only familiar and well-known animals are our animals of strength. Insects and reptiles can serve as transmitters of messages or give us a certain insight that will support us during the rest of our mental and spiritual development. Sometimes, the animal of strength may be an extinct animal (such as the Australian bird, the dodo), a mythological animal (such as the unicorn or Pegasus, the winged horse), or even a centaur (half man and half horse, one of Sagittarius' symbols). Sometimes, it can be an animal that does not exist in any mythology or in any zoological textbook - a unique animal, or an animal from another world.

Meeting the animal of strength

The animal of strength you will meet in this meditation may be the animal you expected - or may not be. You are therefore advised not to have expectations. It is important not to think of a particular animal before beginning the meditation, so that you can be open to all possibilities. If the animal that you imagine to be your animal of strength is indeed your animal of strength during this period of your life, it will appear by itself.

Perform the meditation in a quiet, calm place with quiet and clean energies. Clear your mind of all thoughts. Relax your body. (You can use the Jacobson technique - contracting and relaxing all the muscles from your toes upward, or you can project light onto every organ until you feel totally relaxed.)

Close your eyes. Take two deep, slow breaths. Inhale through your nose and hold your breath as long as you can - without feeling uncomfortable - and exhale through your mouth. Ignore any irrelevant thought that may pop into your mind. Behind your closed eyes, see a white screen. Concentrate on it. You may see some pleasant color or shape beginning to emerge in your mind's eye. In your thoughts, ask your animal of strength to show itself on the screen. Concentrate hard on your request.

Wait patiently and don't let any thoughts distract you. Within a certain amount of time, the image of an animal will appear before your eyes. It may advance slowly toward you, or you may see it in a sharp, clear flash. It may reveal itself from behind, the side, or the front. It may even be an animal that you don't like - don't let this bother you. Let the image emerge in your mind's eye.

The moment you see the animal, look at it quietly, and notice what it is doing, if it is performing any actions. Direct your thoughts to picking up messages telepathically from the animal. These could occur as a voice speaking inside you, as other pictures, or as the intuitive knowledge of the animal's words or messages. As we said before, the message may be in a human language that is familiar to you. Sometimes the animal appears as part of an occurrence or event that is familiar to you. Of course, this situation also bears an individual message.

Concentrate as hard as you can. Notice the colors that surround the animal and then open your eyes slowly. In your heart, thank the universal force for letting you channel with your animal of strength, and write down your experiences and sights in your awareness notebook. You can also draw what you saw. Sometimes it happens that you see more than one animal, or an animal that exists in the real world along with some kind of mythological animal. Similarly, another time, a different animal may appear, bearing a different message.

After the meditation, you should think of the following things: Have you ever dreamed of a particular kind of animal? What happened in that dream? You can ask that animal to appear in your dream at night and channel with it. To this end, you can use crystals for channeling and dreaming. After you have seen the animal in the meditation, ask yourself why that particular animal appeared in front of you.

Messages and insights

There are many animals, each of which has an important message for us. Of course, there are not more important animals or less important animals, but it would take too long to describe the messages of all the animals, so I will present a variety of animals that appear relatively frequently in meditations. If the animal you saw in the meditation does not appear here, you can discover its message very simply - by observation. Get hold of a picture of the animal, or better still, a videotape (by National Geographic, for instance) in which you see the animal in action. Observe it closely, learn its ways, how it copes with problems, how it obtains food, how it raises its young, how it fights or survives, how it walks, its general appearance, its movements - all those are messages that describe the message that the animal wants to convey to you. Another way, no less simple, is just to invite the animal again, but this time ask it to give you the message and describe what it represents.

Carrying a bride over the threshold

The custom of a man carrying his bride over the threshold of the house or of the bedroom is very widespread. The origin of this custom is ancient. In Europe, in poor communities, when there was no money for the couple to pay for a marriage license, the two would hold hands and jump over a broom. This was considered a legal marriage, and they could register as a married couple in the community or church registers.

This custom of jumping over a broom, in conjunction with the conquering male who hits the virginal woman on the head and drags her behind him in order to ravish her, led to the custom of carrying a bride into the house in which her innocence would be deflowered. The bride displays a cautious measure of restraint and reluctance, and the man demonstrates his virility and his strength in a civilized way.

It is an incredibly bad omen for the bride to slip out of the man's arms before he gets her into the house. (Once inside the house, both of them can fall down!) In many cases, this tragic event can even cause the marriage to be annulled. The solution is for one of them to go on a diet, and the other to work out at the gym!

The fact that this custom was thought to be an essential ingredient for future happiness caused many contemporary feminists to oppose it... or to carry their husbands over the threshold!

The animals and the insights they represent

Albatross - Patience; stoicism; endurance; understanding of the importance of long-term parental commitment; ability to remain in emotional states for a long time; uncomfortable, strange, but effective, beginnings and ends.

Ant - Patience; endurance, durability; planning; the necessary energy and patience for completing a task or work; communal life; hoarding for the future.

Anteater - Ability to find lost items; link with the insect world; ability to "sniff out" trouble before seeing it; understanding the value of "digging" for finding solutions.

Antilope - Taking a stand; ability to leap over obstacles; strong survival abilities; speed; gentleness; link to the earth.

Armadillo - Understanding personal boundaries; respecting other people's boundaries; carrying your protection with you at all times and in all situations; understanding your vulnerability and weak spots; empathy; ability to discern.

Baboon - Consecrated to the god Thuth (god of wisdom) and to the god Hepi (god of the Nile); protecting the family.

Badger - Guardian of stories; aggression; biting and courageous self-expression; cunning, deceit; passion; vengefulness, vengeance; stubbornness, persistence; control; antidote to passivity or being a victim; persistence in serving a cause; grounding; knowledge of and familiarity with the earth; charm connected to the earth and the wisdom of the earth; guarding and protecting rights and spiritual ideas.

Bald eagle - Rising up above the material in order to see the spiritual; speed; courage; wisdom; strength; sharp vision; creation; healing; spiritual illumination; knowledge of positive spells and witchcraft; ability to recognize spiritual truths; link to upper truths; ability to see the whole picture; link to spiritual teachers and guides and to soul guides; honor, grace, and goodness; creative and intuitive spirit; tremendous strength and balance; grace and goodness that are attained through knowledge and toil; respect for boundaries of fields and sectors.

Bat - Shamanic death and rebirth; initiation; passage, change; beginning of new ideas; seeing previous lives; understanding sorrow; camouflage; ability to see the invisible; use of sound vibrations;

Bear - Looking inward; healing; loneliness/solitude; change; link with the wind; death and rebirth; astral travel; transformation; production of dreams, shamans and mystics; man of vision; protection and vengeance; wisdom.

Beaver - Persistence, industriousness; preserving the ability to be productive in all ways by not limiting one's options; using existing resources; using various methods for accomplishing tasks; master builder of all things; understanding the dynamics of group work; not stopping the flow of experiences in life; achievements stemming from the completion of tasks.

Bee - Prosperity; concentration; understanding the energy of the female fighter; reincarnation; communication with the dead; helping the spirits that are still tied to the earth to move onward to their appropriate place.

Black panther - Astral travel; protective energy; symbol of femininity; understanding death; death and rebirth; ability to acknowledge darkness; restoration of personal forces that were taken away.

Buffalo / Bison - Abundance; feminine courage; creativity connected to the earth; knowledge; generosity; hospitality; courage; collaboration; strength; challenge; survival; giving for the good of others; developing beneficial plans.

Butterfly / Caterpillar - Strength of the storm and air turbulence; transformation; reincarnation; spell/witchcraft; change.

Buzzard - Helps in healing the soul; accompanies the soul back to the world of the souls; the study of speed and agility; control of speed and movement; learning the tricks of life; understanding spells.

Camel - Transformation of the loads we carry; ability to save for future use; understanding the open spaces; learning to walk through the shifting sands of time.

Canary - Beautiful voice; use of song for healing; finding the song of the soul; happiness; ability to find happiness in song in times of darkness and shadow.

Cat - Independence; seeing the invisible; protection; enables us to dream our dreams; love; helps in meditations; ability to fight when pushed into a corner.

Centipede - Coordination; balance; ability to survive at times of pressure and hardship; beauty of movement.

Chameleon - Use of the sun as a source of power; ability to climb up high in order to accomplish objectives; patience; use of color for camouflage; pulling things toward you as a means of survival.

Cheetah - Brotherhood; evasiveness; ability to focus on one thing intensely for a short time; agility and speed; self-esteem; hurrying, sense of time; sharpness of vision.

Chimpanzee - Linguistic abilities; understanding the complexities of society; wisdom; link with the spirits of the forest; solution to problems; skill; ability to balance between aggression and compassion.

Cobra - Soul guide; memory of the world of the soul; memories of previous lives; the wisdom of divine female energy; transformation of the soul; freedom from religious persecutions.

Cockroach - Understanding loathing and revulsion in other people; passage through fear; understanding shadows; speed for the sake of escaping injury.

Coral - Providing a living environment for everything; symbiosis; understanding the need for variety; community life, communal life.

Cormorant - Patience; ability to grasp the essentials; use of the sun as a healing power.

Cow - Love; alertness to danger; satisfaction; link to expanses of green grass; ability to share that is expressed in community life; ability to stand up for oneself.

Crab - Understanding the power of dance; ability to escape by moving sideways; ability to pass through water (emotions); finding new uses for what seems unusable; the masculine aspects of the community; protecting the domestic space.

Crane - Symbol of light and spring; astral travel; longevity; new knowledge; elegance; seeks to help others along their path; wisdom; ability to see all the things that are connected to secrets; unique use of the voice.

Cricket - Finding the way out of the dark by following the personal song; good luck; teaches the power of song in times of darkness; understanding the correct timing to jump out of a particular situation; communication; connection with the plant kingdom.

Crocodile - Maternal protection; link to Mother Earth; protection against manipulations; initiation; vengeance through tolerance; ability to spot deception and cunning; understanding the weather; entry into ancient knowledge.

Crow - Rebirth; renewal; recovery; cycle; healing (return and recovery of lost parts of the soul); casting light on shadow; link-up to the source; reflections/mirrors; self-acceptance; introspection; finding consolation in solitude; honoring the ancient fathers; the spells of the elders; prediction of the future; change in awareness; new occurrences; purity of language.

Cuckoo - Efficiency; ability to adapt; new beginnings; meeting with personal destiny.

Deer - Ability to listen; grace and appreciation of beauty and equilibrium; gentleness of touch, speech, and thought; understanding what is required for survival; power; gratitude and giving; ability to sacrifice oneself for lofty objectives; finding alternative routes to the objective.

Dingo - Human soul that was reborn (possibility); tracking and scouting talents; assistance in hunting; finding warmth in cold situations; loyalty; understanding silence; finding the truth; friendship; protection; correct use of intuition; ability to resign oneself.

Dog - Heals emotional wounds in human beings; companionship, friendship; complete loyalty; unconditional love; understanding the duality of belief and doubt; knowledge of all the sensual things and those that are linked to the senses; protection; ability to "sniff out" trouble from afar.

Dolphin - Gift of God; knowledge of the sea; patron of seafarers; change; balance; trust; harmony; communicative abilities; freedom; wisdom; understanding the power of rhythms in personal life; use of the breath to release repressed or oppressive emotions; spells linked to the element of water.

Donkey - Obstinacy; ability to carry out decisions; saying "no" to other people; objection to taking steps that the person knows are not right for him; ignoring other people's opinions.

Dove / Turtledove / Wild pigeon - Brings peace and love; messenger of the spirit; communication between two worlds; understanding pleasantness and gentleness.

Dragonfly - Shattering of illusions; life's secrets in flight; the force of flight; understanding dreams; ability to escape in a flash; seeing the truth in situations; agility and speed; change; link to the dragon.

Duck - Water energy (emotional energy); ability to see clearly through emotions; grace in water; helps mystics and visionaries spiritually.

Eagle (American) / Falcon / Condor - Death and rebirth; prophecy; purifying and self-purification; new vision; love of the spirit of God; knowledge concerning the death of a loved one.

Eel - Power of electricity; camouflage; ability to observe the invisible; fleeing when threatened.

Elephant - Strength; regality; confidence; connection to ancient wisdom; taking advantage of the possibilities to study and enrich one's knowledge; patience; lack of barriers, boundaries, and obstacles.

Finch - Creating balance in relations with various people; understanding the value of change; ability to resolve family conflicts in an effective and healthy way; understanding the power of the voice.

Firefly - Ability to find the light in the darkness; use of light for communication; ability to channel with colors.

Fish - Abundance; fertility; children; harmony; love; renewal; balance between reason and emotion.

Flamingo - Understanding the language of colors; ability to preserve the purpose of the soul in group life; understanding how to preserve equilibrium; ability to sieve the lessons of the soul out of the emotional waters.

Fox - Change of shape; smartness; ability to look out and observe; cunning; stealth, moving secretly; camouflage; feminine courage; ability to be invisible; ability to see the invisible; persistence; gentleness; agility.

Frog - Reminds us of the link that exists with all the life in the universe; cleansing and purification; transformation; singing songs that celebrate the beginning of the ancient water sources; rebirth; understanding emotions.

Giraffe - Intuition; communication; ability to reach things that others cannot reach; ability to look into the distant future; ability to lift oneself and remain above quarrels and friction.

Goat, billy-goat - Abundance; independence; search for new heights; confidence, no stumbling; discarding guilt feelings; understanding the creatures and energies of nature; lightness of movement;

Goldfish - Prophecy; harmony; beauty; peace; balance between reason and emotion.

Gorilla - Wisdom, intelligence; gentleness; maternal instincts; generosity; verbal and oratorial ability.

Goose - Happiness; walking along the path of the soul; understanding the strength of the community; helping others in times of trouble or illness.

Hare - Quick-thinking; receiving hidden and intuitive messages; deception, trickery; paradoxes and contradictions; living according to personal wisdom; humility; the ability to move through fear; strengthening the intuition.

Hawk - Deliverer of spiritual messages; sharp powers of discrimination; ability to be an observer of what is happening; long-term memory; remembering previous lives; wisdom; guardianship; courage; enlightenment; seeing the whole picture; creativity; truth; experience; overcoming problems; ability to make use of opportunities wisely.

Hedgehog - Innocence; confidence in the spirit; creating one's personal path; ability to let others follow their personal paths without interfering; renewal of the sense of wonder and of the miraculous in life; maintaining boundaries; protecting oneself when threatened; non-disturbance/non-interference.

Hen / Rooster - Hearing the inner voice/listening to your inner voice; picking up the answers that others cannot grasp; powers that awake with sunrise; power of the voice; understanding the language; protecting the family and the community.

Heron - Confidence in the self, ability to rely on the self; boundaries; self-esteem; juggling multiple tasks; colorfulness; honor, nobility.

Hippopotamus - Correct use of aggressions; can move gracefully through the emotions; protecting the family; the birth of new ideas; maternal rage when necessary.

Horse / Pony / Mustang - Power, strength; endurance and tolerance; devotion; awareness of the power that is attained through true cooperation; broadening the potential abilities; dominance and control over the environment; the liberty to gallop freely; hikes and journeys; astral travel; patron of hikers; communication between different species; warning of possible danger; guide to overcoming obstacles.

Hummingbird - Merriment; love; happiness; ability to heal by using light as a laser beam from the mouth; endurance on long journeys; ability to fly to small (hidden) places in order to heal oneself.

Hyena - Knowledge of the secrets of the wild; ability to adapt; understanding how to control epidemics; strength; understanding the value of cooperation; patience; singing the personal song of the soul; persistence in hunting; connection with the vulture; defense of borders; communication in dark regions; understanding the importance of life in the community.

Ibis - Understanding ancient wisdom; contact with the Egyptian gods; wisdom; enlightenment; the ability to work with sorcerers.

Jackal - Astral travel; access to previous lives; understanding the use of opportunities; ability to see in the dark (spiritual darkness, too); link to the Egyptian pyramids; link to the constellation Orion.

Jaguar - Extrasensory vision; moving fearlessly in the dark; seeing the paths in chaos; understanding the patterns of chaos; promoting the soul's work; empowering the self; movement in unknown places; change of shape.

Kangaroo - Protecting the young; creating a safe domestic environment; leaping far from problematic and negative situations; ability to adapt to new situations.

Kingfisher - Peace; happiness and love; link to the pacific seas (and oceans)/emotional tranquillity; bright and clear observation through emotional waters, and extracting your dream from them.

Kiwi - Link to the ancient wisdom of the enlightened; understanding the earth's changes; ability to "scratch" the truth out.

Koala - Ability to climb over obstacles; understanding the value of slow movement; the power of Yoga; gives useful advice; ability to remain aloof from brawls and disagreements.

Leopard - Strength; energetic; marvelous sense of timing; acting without prior analytical thinking; strength and willpower in the face of trouble and hardship.

Lemur - Seeing the invisible; access to knowledge of forests; ability to navigate through forests; understanding the ability to remain above the vicissitudes of life; ability to grasp ideas that are beyond the static nature of life.

Lion - Brotherhood; courage; energy; power and strength; relieving pressure and burdens; strong family ties; self-realization.

Lizard - Separations from the ego; coping with fears; ability to control dreams; movement in other worlds; ability to revive or renew things that have withered or gotten lost.

Llama / Guanaco / Vicuna (South American camel) - Consoling others; passing over hedges; ability to tolerate and survive the cold; overcoming materialism.

Locust / Grasshopper - Astral travel; leap of faith; jumping over time and space; jumping without knowing where you'll land; jumping over obstacles; new leaps forward; ability to change professions swiftly.

Marten - Fearlessness in self-defense and attack; stopping people who do evil/fear of people who do injustice; protecting the family; using speed for protection.

Medusa - Sensitivity to the energy of the element of water - emotions; understanding the value of floating while swimming at difficult emotional times and during emotional trials; correct use of softness; ability to disentangle oneself from the web of life's dangers.

Mole - Guards the low places; linked to the energies of the earth; knowledge of plants, roots, minerals, seeds, and hidden rivers and minerals of the earth; the ability to withdraw into oneself; introspection, being blind to everything in the material world by seeing light and dark only; natural love; sensitivity to touch and vibrations; understanding the energies and their ways of flowing.

Monkey - Movement through the ego; understanding success; good health; ability to change one's surroundings; protecting the family; understanding situations of excess and exaggeration.

Mosquito - Use of water for transformation/use of emotions for transformation; directing the energy flow in one direction; pulling energy inward.

Moth - Power of the storm; slow movement in the dark, in the shadows; ability to find light in the darkness; ability to confuse enemies; transformation.

Mouse / Lemming / Rat - Understanding fine details; examining the lesson of life; quiet; diffidence; invisibility; seeing the double meaning of things; ability to be stealthy; guide when signing contracts; discovery and revelation; ability to be invisible.

Nightingale - Correct use of song for healing; use of song for passing beyond fears; link with the moon; use of vibratory energy for seeing between the shadows.

Octopus / Squid / Ink-fish - Wisdom; destruction of negative barriers; fast movement to get away from danger when necessary; correct use of a smokescreen in order to escape from enemies.

Orang-utan - Gentleness; link with the spirits of the forest; movement above quarrels and disagreements; wit and inventiveness when coping with problems.

Ostrich - Help in expelling evil spirits; spiritual truth; understanding all aspects of denial; evasiveness, abstemious behavior; ability to outrun rivals; community life.

Otter - Feminine energy; the feminine healing wisdom; sensitivity and fineness of feelings without suspicions; guide to discovering and removing the masks covering abilities and talents; extrasensory awareness; faith; matters concerning recovery (physical or emotional); understanding the value of play and fun.

Owl - Secrecy; fast and silent movement; ability to be

stealthy; ability to see behind the masks; sharp vision; messenger for signs and secrets; change of shape; link between the dark and the invisible world on the one hand, and the world of light on the other; ability to accept the shadows in our personality; spells and witchcraft regarding the moon; freedom.

Oyster - Understanding when to close doors in order to avoid losing energy; ability to filter out the static aspects of life; maintaining strong and enduring external defense; sensitivity to environmental changes.

Panda - Understanding the value of slow motion; balance; ability to adapt; link to Eastern art; link to the plant kingdom.

Parakeet - Love; imitation, mimicry; ability to change direction abruptly; trust; helps with objectives concerning the community.

Parrot - Use of language; relationship between the members of a couple; imitation; brings rain; wisdom and guidance to think before speaking.

Peacock - All the aspects of beauty; immortality; honor; ability to see into the past, present, and future; self-confidence; ability to get up after suffering a heavy blow.

Pelican - Control of the ego; correct use of abundance; ability to float through emotions; recovery from loss; ability to return from being on the verge of extinction.

Penguin - Paternity; understanding the feminine energy in the male; patience; astral travel; daydreams; endurance.

Pheasant / Partridge - Movement beyond the ego; use of color for healing purposes; development and broadening of the self-awareness; understanding the use of ceremonies.

Pig - Knowledge of previous lives; strong earth spell/enchantment; wisdom; cunning; becoming invisible when in danger.

Polar bear - Ability to navigate along all the magnetic lines of the earth; solitude/loneliness; introspection; expertise at swimming through the waters of the emotions; ability to find possibilities of a livelihood in desolate expanses; finding the way back from the brink; dreams; death and rebirth; production of dreams, shamans, mystics, and visionaries; transformation; strength in times of trouble; channeling with the spirit; protection and vengeance.

Porcupine - Protection against negativity; fertility; enjoyment of life; the wisdom of old women; understanding weather patterns.

Prairie wolf / Coyote - Wisdom, intelligence; ability to laugh at our mistakes; change of shape; learning the balance between safety and risk; understanding that all things are sacred, but, having said that, nothing is sacred; learning that only when all the masks have been removed can we link up to the source; song of praise to the Creation; innocent belief in the truth; teaches us how to raise our young ones (children, the inner child); rainmaker; enlightenment; ability to be stealthy.

Praying mantis - Ability to maneuver time; ability to move between moments; ability to remain motionless and silent; understanding the circular nature of time; feminine fighting energies; attack strategies.

Puma / Cougar / Mountain lion - Leadership and charisma; wise, use of the power of leadership without ego; equilibrium between strength, intention, and ability; accumulation of self-confidence; liberation from guilt feelings; cunning.

Quail - Life close to the earth; ability to fade into the background; courage to cope with hard labor; finding peaceful solutions to dangerous situations.

Rat - Protection, defense; sign of fertility and wealth; creation of abundance; wisdom and intelligence; ability to be invisible; ability to be stealthy.

Rhinoceros - Learning the ability to console oneself in situations of loneliness; link to ancient wisdom; wise use of ancient wisdom; knowing oneself; confidence in one's instincts.

Robin - Paternity; courting; an understanding of the strength of the blowing wind; finding the song of your soul.

Salamander -Link to the soul's memory of early days on earth; promoting the connection between earth and water; change; encouragement in the dark; ability to put on a disguise in the face of danger.

Salmon - The value of returning home in order to renew one's forces; swimming on top of the current of emotions in order to achieve new insights; rebirth of spiral knowledge; understanding the messages of fortune-telling.

Scorpion - Death and rebirth; transformation (change of form) of poison; returning dark and negative energy to the sender.

Seagull - Spiritual messenger; channeling; friendship; ability to look at the situation from above; responsible behavior.

Seal - Movement through emotions; protection when changes are occurring; lucid dreams; protection against danger; creativity.

Shark - Ability to live in the here and now; self-acceptance and spiritual, emotional, and physical acceptance; ability to move frequently; work/movement in silence; "devours" negative energy; recycling of energy; link to the past; a living fossil - a living organism while the species closest to it have become extinct; cruelty, ruthlessness; never caught unprepared; ability to defend oneself.

Sheep / Ewe / Ram - New beginnings; maintaining balance in dangerous situations; fertility; confidence in one's abilities; courage needed for maintaining balance; abundance; feeling of confidence in new places and fields.

Skunk - Self-respect; reputation; sensuality; willpower; understanding of how to "do your own thing"; courage; self-confidence.

Sloth - Understanding the spirits of the trees; the value of laziness; the wisdom connected to slow movement; the ability to enter spheres in the trees that contain all the knowledge of the earth; observing the world upside-down; ability to understand when to stick to your guns and not give up.

Snail - Ability to use slow movement as an advantage or for gaining benefit; the importance of being ambulatory; understanding the importance of leaving a trail behind you; understanding the value of humor; protection by means of retreat; sensuality.

Snake - Messenger of the rainbow snake (according to the Native American and Aborigine tradition); slipperiness; revelation of the mysteries of life; activates lightning (according to the Native American tradition); change of shape; ancient and elemental energy; guarding against religious persecutions; extrasensory energy; creative force; immortality; serves the shaman as a magic rope to the world of the souls.

Sparrow - Fertility; passion; discovery of new love in life; ability to use the power of song; understanding the different aspects of race; all the aspects of color.

Spider - Master weaver; weaves the webs of fate; wisdom; creativity; divine inspiration; change of shape; understanding the patterns of illusion; feminine energy for the creative life force.

Squirrel - Quick change of direction; resourcefulness; change; revelation; ability to solve puzzles and problems; hoarding for the future; balance between giving and receiving; warning; avoiding danger by climbing up to high places.

Starling - Imitation, mimicry; adaptiveness; ability to control crowds; wisdom, intelligence; mental reception and absorption.

Stork - Creativity; new beginnings; protecting the young; fidelity, devotion.

Swallow - Proximity to the legendary thunderbird; strength of life in the community, in a group; understanding the value of family and home; protection; maneuverability; agility, lightness of movement; a sign of spring (emotional).

Swan - Stimulating the inner strength; understanding of dream symbols; looking into the future; predicting the future; pleasantness and grace in relations with others; developing intuitive abilities.

Tick - Disseminating ideas; trickery, sophistication; ability to use warmth and movement in order to see; patience.

Tit - Lack of fear; standing; ability to wear crowns without ego; the power of the voice.

Toucan - Ease of movement, agility; skill; ability to move to and from the world of the souls; correct use of healing colors; ability to find tranquillity in small places.

Toad - Link to different states of awareness; symbol of the earth; change of luck; long life; camouflage of poison.

Turkey - Self-sacrifice for a lofty cause; understanding the gift of giving; respecting Mother Earth; winning prizes.

Turtle - Symbol of the earth; link to the center; patience; ability to navigate; personal boundaries; link to the feminine; development of new ideas; ability to cure feminine diseases; respect for other people's boundaries; ability to protect oneself spiritually; self-reliance; non-violent protection; stubbornness, taking root.

Wasp - Using the energy of feminine warfare; sisterhood; community life; understanding female friendship.

Weasel - Ability to be stealthy; power of discernment, and sharp discernment; slyness; vengeance; trickery; ability to see the hidden reasons behind things.

Whale - Guardian of knowledge; all the knowledge concerning the voice; beauty and movement; extrasensory and telepathic ability; all the aspects of the sea.

Wild boar - Courage; protection; use of the mask of rage; ability to sense danger; ability to find the truth.

Wildcat - Developing the extrasensory senses; sharp vision (sensory and extrasensory); predicting the future; keeping all secrets and mysteries; movement through time and space.

Wild rooster - Stands at the opening of the big spiral; understanding the cyclical nature of time; understanding of and work with circles and cycles; knows how to move through the big spiral; dances the sanctified dance of life.

Woodpecker - Link to the earth; ability to discover hidden layers; understanding rhythms, patterns, and cycles; prophecy; drummer of the earth; linked to thunder; warnings.

Wolf - Death and rebirth; facing the end of the personal life cycle with courage and honor; spiritual study; guide in dreaming and meditation; instincts linked to intelligence; social and family values; tricking and defeating enemies; the ability to go without being seen; stability, permanence; ability to protect the self and the family; ability to exploit changes positively.

Worm / Earthworm - Regeneration, renewal; purification of the earth; ability to find nutrition in the depths of the earth; camouflage.

Zebra - Balance; confidence in the route; seeing black and white; brightness without filters; strength; maintaining individuality in the herd.

Amulet

Amulets, in general, are objects whose purpose is to stop evil and promote good. The amulet must be kept within the field of action of good or evil, since its range of operation is limited. (For this reason, an amulet is carried on the person, or is placed at the entrance to the house, and so on.)

There is a difference between a "natural" amulet and a man-made one.

A natural amulet is in fact an everyday object that, in addition to its regular use, is also used as an amulet - a horseshoe, for instance. Sometimes it is part of a whole body or object, such as a rabbit's foot or a rhinoceros horn, and so on.

A man-made amulet is an object that is manufactured to serve specifically as an amulet. When we write on parchment, as in a mezuzah scroll, for instance, or hang a hamsa (a hand) on a chain - this is an amulet that we define as man-made.

There are amulets that combine sound and form, such as a bell that hangs at the entrance to a house, or a whistle on the roof through which the wind whistles. Other amulets make use of certain odors - usually perfumes.

Color is extremely important, as is the material from which the amulet is made. A horseshoe must be made of iron, but a bell made of gold will be "stronger" than one made of iron.

There are many amulets that come from the plant or animal world - red pepper, for instance, is a very common amulet against the evil eye. Various birds and fish are good luck amulets.

Many superstitions are linked to amulets, and the number of amulets in the various cultures is as large as the number of superstitions.

Pyramid

The pyramid, known to us primarily from ancient Egypt, appears in many beliefs - both because of its complicated and powerful structure, and because the pyramid is one of the most stable structures that man can build.

A pyramid made from three iron nails often served as an amulet at the entrance to the house, similar to a horseshoe.

The pyramid structure is thought to nourish body and soul, and fortify fertility and virility. That is why many people sleep under a pyramid-shaped canopy, or build a pyramid-shaped room in their home.

There is a belief that food that is placed in a pyramid never goes off.

Conclusion

As you read these concluding words, I imagine that you know a lot more about wicca. Even so, the question, "What is wicca?" still exists.

When I planned this book, the list of chapters included dozens of topics - for instance, dreams, the most important topic in the work of the wicca practitioner; crystals - the gifts of Mother Earth; topics that are not presented in this book, as well as topics that especially interest the reader, such as the connection between wicca and love - a topic that grew and grew until it became a self-standing book (*The WIcca of Love*), which has already been published. The problem was not what to add to the book. The problem I faced was shortening and sifting, and still keeping the basic principles of wicca.

"Do something simple," was the advice of the editors at the publishing house that publishes my books. "Think of the book as a new wicca group that includes people who have no idea about wicca. What would you teach them during their first three months in the group? What would you want them to know as they approach their first initiation ceremony?"

I took his advice. This book contains rays of light that illuminate the areas of wicca that are the most important to the wicca practitioner, **in my eyes**. I am aware of the fact that the emphasis may be different in other wicca groups or books, but that is the nature of wicca.So long as the fundamental principles are adhered to, everyone can find a corner that suits them in the infinite realm of wicca's manifestations in everyday life.

ASTROLOG COMPLETE GUIDES SERIES